The Night was a Bright Moonlight and I Could See a Man Quite Plain

An Edwardian Cricket Murder

The Night was a Bright Moonlight and I Could See a Man Quite Plain

An Edwardian Cricket Murder

GIDEON HAIGH

SCRIBNER

SCRIBNER

First published in Australia in 2022 by Gideon Haigh
This edition published in Australia in 2022 by Scribner,
an imprint of Simon & Schuster Australia
Suite 19A, Level 1, Building C, 450 Miller Street, Cammeray, NSW 2062

Sydney New York London Toronto New Delhi
Visit our website at www.simonandschuster.com.au

10 9 8 7 6 5 4 3 2

© Gideon Haigh 2022

A catalogue record for this
book is available from the
National Library of Australia

9781761108266 (paperback)
9781761108273 (ebook)

Cover and interior design by Anne-Marie Reeves
Cover images from Queensland State Archives
Typeset in Adobe Jenson Pro
Printed and bound in Australia by Griffin Press

The paper this book is printed on is certified against the Forest
Stewardship Council® Standards. Griffin Press holds FSC®
chain of custody certification SGSHK-COC-005088.
FSC® promotes environmentally responsible, socially beneficial
and economically viable management of the world's forests.

CONTENTS

Books are apt to beget other books. Early in 2021, I was re-reading Cyril Pearl's *Morrison of Peking*, a biography of the Sinophile, when I noted a sentence concerning a 1919 letter to G. E. Morrison from his masseur Arthur Robertson: 'Mr Robertson, who was a great gossip, told Morrison that G. F. Vernon, one of the Ivo Bligh team of cricketers, had a son, a man of violent temper, who in a fit of jealousy had murdered a white companion on a Queensland station, smashing his head with a cricket bat.' Hmmm. Interesting. Before moving on, I dog-eared the page as worth returning to.

Some years earlier, I had read Clive Powell-Williams's *Cold Burial* about the reckless polar explorer Jack Hornby, son of A. N. 'Monkey' Hornby, England's captain at the Oval 1882. I'd wondered then about the children of those eminent Victorian cricketers, those who'd followed their fathers and those who had not. G. F. Vernon had sailed to Australia just weeks after that epoch-making Test to retrieve the Ashes lost by Hornby's team. The XI, famously led by the Hon Ivo Bligh, had met with signal success. But who was his son, and why had he taken up a cricket bat to such a different end? Opportunity to investigate presented itself as 2021 degenerated into a recycled 2020, and I wearied of describing cricket matches I couldn't attend and cricket personalities I could not meet. Studying 1911 was certainly more fun than enduring Dan Andrews one hundred and ten years later. A short book was called for, which I hope you enjoy.

GIDEON HAIGH
September 2021

PROLOGUE

On the afternoon of Friday 21 July 1911, a young man bearing a bundle of papers knocked on the frosted glass of an upstairs door in Odhams House in Long Acre. Eyes turned as he entered. When someone arrived at *John Bull*, London's most salacious weekly, it could mean anything. They might be remonstrating about a libel; they might be complaining of an injustice; an asylum inmate once arrived brandishing a razor. Regularly the visitors were process servers, acting for the numerous creditors of its financier proprietor Horatio Bottomley MP – against him, over the years, more than 250 petitions for bankruptcy were filed. The offices had been configured with this in mind. The door with the brass plate reading 'Mr Bottomley' opened to an empty bogey hole; Bottomley's actual lair was behind this, separated by another locked door. Thus could especially importunate visitors be parked while Bottomley slipped down a back stairway out an emergency exit fifty metres down Anne Street.

George Vernon

Horatio Bottomley MP

This visitor seemed harmless enough, and it happened that the edition had gone to press, so a private secretary admitted him to the editor's plush inner sanctum, all oak partitions and green leather. On one wall was a framed copy of the first *John Bull* front page, showing the English archetype in the company of a lugubrious bulldog; on another was an image of The Dicker, the editor's country retreat. Rows of black deed boxes lettered in gold bore the names of legal adversaries, albeit that these were mainly for show, being mostly empty. On the mantelpiece was a life-sized cream bust of the late Charles Bradlaugh MP, the militant atheist, secularist, republican and free thinker – Bottomley took pleasure in the widespread rumour, almost certainly false, that Bradlaugh was his father. On the desk was a photograph of the man himself, posing heroically with a sheaf of papers in hand, as though proclaiming the publication's motto: 'If you read it in *John Bull*, it is so.'

Behind the desk, fleshy and imperious, reposed Bottomley. He was a man capable of great magnanimity and utter unscrupulousness. Once a worker who had lost his legs in a lift accident hobbled all the way from Dulwich on two sticks to tell his story. Bottomley gave him two pounds, had his chauffeur drive him home, and pursued the story until it was satisfactorily resolved. On another occasion, he was visited by a well-known peer who having been made a minister of the crown suddenly craved popularity. Bottomley held his hand out: 'How popular would his lordship like to be?' Better at making money than keeping it, Bottomley was prone to quixotic generosity. Told by his assistant that a favourite railway attendant of his was in prison, he responded: 'Why, we must send money to his wife at once.' Advised that the man was in prison for bigamy, he adjusted: 'Well, we must send money to both his wives.'

Bottomley now sought to appraise his visitor, who introduced himself as George Vernon. He was short, stocky, brown-haired, clean-shaven, well-attired, in his mid-twenties. His accent located him among the well-to-do. So Bottomley was surprised when George Vernon divulged the reason for his visit. The reason was murder.

Surprised, and also delighted. Bottomley liked murder. Before *John Bull*, he had owned London's *Sun*, turning it from a rather staid and sober news sheet into something more popular and, for the times, vulgar. Its approach to violent crime was often original. Bottomley opened an appeal for the daughter of Bennett the Yarmouth murderer, whom he had made a ward in chancery after her father's execution; he fought to save Gardner the alleged Peasenhall murderer from a triple jeopardy trial, after two hung juries. On the day in July 1903 when Samuel Dougal, the Moat Farm murderer, was hanged at Chelmsford Prison, the *Sun* printed a facsimile of his confession — nobody knew if it was genuine but, of course, its authorship could no longer be challenged.

Most notoriously, in September 1910, *John Bull* had pulled off the coup of publishing a confession by the infamous poisoner Dr Crippen, although its provenance had quickly become controversial. Bottomley had been surreptitiously subsidising Crippen's defence on the understanding that *John Bull* would receive the accused's final testament exclusively. 'Brother, how came you to do it?' Bottomley asked Crippen by letter. 'What demon possessed you? Relieve your burning brain, confiding to me the name of your accomplice.' But when the plan had been thwarted by the prison governor, Bottomley had dictated a 'confession' himself.

Crippen's solicitor Arthur Newton had just been suspended from the rolls for attesting the confession's veracity; Bottomley, unpunished and unchastened, now seemed to be in proximity to another such story. Was it true? Was it false? Did this matter? When the young man explained that he wished to make a statement, Bottomley excitedly took up his pen. His first job had been as a court stenographer; he had excellent shorthand. Giving his name as George Valentine Jeffray Vernon, the visitor commenced: 'I am the son of the well-known Middlesex cricketer. I was at the time I speak of under twenty-five years of age. My life had been a stormy one...'

1

'A HARD MAN'

On the face of it, George Vernon's life should not have been stormy at all. On the contrary, he had been born with what appeared a host of advantages, including the patrimony to which he drew Bottomley's attention. George grew up idolising his father and adoring his mother – and not without good reason.

That father, George Frederick Vernon, was known all his life, in newspapers and correspondence alike, by his brisk, brusque, businesslike initials, G. F. He was the beau ideal of an English amateur athlete. He was tall, lean and active. He shot, fished and hunted. He was hard to beat at racquets and billiards. He played the eponymous sport of his school, Rugby, well enough to enjoy a long career at Ravenscourt and Blackheath, and to earn five caps for England as a nimble forward. Above all was G. F. a cricketer, an enterprising batsman and earnest competitor, stern and unsmiling in every photograph, individual and joint, that survives from his lengthy first-class career. 'He was a hard man, but he loved music and his Yorkshire terrier dog,' recalled Lord Hawke in his memoirs. It is a slightly strained tribute, as though reaching for qualities to excuse someone's general severity – and Hawke, Yorkshire's great martinet of amateurism, who famously prayed that England should never stoop so low as to be captained by a professional cricketer, was scarcely one to bestow the tag of 'hard' lightly.

G.F. Vernon

G. F. was born in Marylebone on 20 June 1856, the only son of an artillery captain who had served in India, George, and his wife, Emily nee Speer. He grew up in the environs of Lewisham and Greenwich, and attended Yverdon House in Blackheath, where he was captain of the XI. He also excelled at cricket when he entered Rugby in September 1870, and the school's records are a pageant of his triumphs, climaxing in his leading the school to victory at Lord's against Marlborough, their traditional rivals. He belonged to that generation of amateurs, before the regular publication of averages, who scorned the acquisition of runs for the sake of style. The scrivener of *Cricket: A Weekly Record*, W. A. Bettesworth, commented approvingly: 'To see Mr Vernon well set at the wickets is one of the greatest pleasures which can fall to the lot of a cricketer.' Boldness redeemed a certain unsoundness: 'For hard and clear hitting it would not have been easy to find Mr Vernon's equal. He relies greatly on a keen eye, and the angle of his bat when he played the ball would have seemed positively shocking to a school coach.'

Biographical data on G. F. is limited. We know that at eighteen he joined the freemasons, that at nineteen both his parents were dead, that at twenty-three he was called to the Honourable Society of the Middle Temple. Cricket, mainly for Middlesex and the Gentlemen, soon eclipsed other distractions, though his record was merely respectable until an extraordinary two days in September 1882 when G. F. put on 605 for the second wicket with A. H. Trevor for the Orleans Club, a pedigree amateur outfit, against an unlucky mob called Rickling Green. Vernon made 259 and Trevor 338 in an all out score of 929, not quite ten times their hosts' total. It was the biggest partnership in the biggest innings total in history, and prompted Vernon's recruitment by the Hon Ivo Bligh for a majority-amateur tour of Australia – that and Vernon's good breeding, public school background and field sport aptitude.

The tour became the *fons et origo* of the Ashes. But it was also a kind of social breakthrough for the colonies. These were not the workaday English professionals of 1876-77 who had played in the inaugural Test match; Bligh's men represented the cream of English sporting society. As one Australian newspaper introduced them on arrival: 'They are a genial, gentlemanly set of men, who put no 'haw-haw' airs on, and who can play cricket. Rich bachelors are included in the team...'

A love match was therefore almost fore-ordained. Bligh fell for Florence Morphy, the companion of Lady Janet Clarke, to whose husband Sir William's Rupertswood estate the amateurs paid regular guest visits – including the fabled occasion on which the Ashes were created as a token for a muck-up game in December 1882. Vernon enjoyed only moderate on-field success, but was sufficiently enamoured of Australia to remain for two months after the tour, and to return to Australia the following summer – some thought permanently. Rockhampton's *Morning Bulletin* reported that 'G. F. Vernon, the cricketer intends to engage in pastoral pursuits in Queensland.' The *Sydney Mail* then reported that 'it is considered likely that Mr Vernon will take up his residence in Victoria.' Vernon was certainly conspicuous as groomsman at the Bligh-Morphy wedding, the social event of the Melbourne season, on 11

February 1884, with its 200 guests arriving by steam train, for a lush ceremony at Sunbury's St Mary's and lavish reception at Rupertswood – an event that uniquely commingled the *beau monde* of England and colonies. The Clarkes, probably Australia's wealthiest family, had invested heavily in lifting Florence onto a social level nearer par with Bligh, in line to inherit the earldom of Darnley. Vernon's fellow groomsmen were Walter Clarke Warrington, private secretary to the governor of Fiji, and Lord William Beaudromp Neville, son of the Marquis of Abergavenny and a former aide-de-camp to the Viceroy of Ireland. Though a very minor peer at home, Neville had since coming to the colonies for his health achieved the status of a social lion. 'He is a tall, graceful, but somewhat delicate young fellow, with an expressive, kindly, and intelligent face,' reported the *Town and Country Journal*. 'He has visited a number of estates in Victoria, and been well pleased with his observations.'

Vernon gave a toast at the wedding on behalf of Bligh's former cricket comrades, and it was all very plush and jolly, with much talk in the speeches of Bligh having made a 'wonderful catch' and a 'winning match', and Lady Clarke's uncle complaining light-heartedly that such events would make it difficult to lure English cricket teams to Australia. 'It was easy enough to get professional players, but the mothers of the gentlemen cricketers put their veto against their sons coming to Australia on the score that they would be sure to bring home a Victorian wife,' he said. 'Then he told of a conversation he had with an English cricketer belonging to the last team, who declared that the reason they all lost their hearts to Australian girls was because they were so unsophisticated.'

One wonders if this was Vernon, because it was on what he would set his heart – marrying one of Florence Morphy's bridesmaids. It's probable Vernon was engaged to comely twenty-two-year-old Marion Jeffray before returning to England; they went to the altar two months after the *Clyde* brought him back to Melbourne in January 1885. Like Bligh's, Vernon-Jeffray was an advantageous union, the groom offering social cachet, the bride financial security. For the Jeffrays were wealthy.

Patriarch Robert, the son of a Dumfries clergyman, had prospered in the colonies as a stock and station agent, and loved cricket, supporting a local club team, Devorgilla, for whom Vernon turned out. Scots Church was the scene, rural money the theme as the couple wed on 3 March 1885. 'Talk about wool kings,' said the *Sydney Mail*, 'the church was crowded with them, to say nothing about the wool queens and the wool princesses. Everybody was very gorgeous, downwards from the bride, who was literally a blaze of diamonds.' On the last of several such engagements, the ubiquitous Lord William Nevill was again the best man – there is the hint here, indeed, of something slightly more.

The following month, Nevill unexpectedly quit the colony, bound for Rome, where he converted to Roman Catholicism, amid talk he would join a monastery and/or take holy orders. Rumour had it that Nevill had been 'deeply smitten' with a Melbourne girl who had gone and 'married the scion of another noble house', leaving him bereft – it's not unlikely that the girl was the blue-eyed charmer Marion Jeffray. Nevill would not be down long. Although estranged from his father by his religious vagrancy, he zeroed in on another wealthy bride – the daughter of a Spanish banker who would bankroll Nevill's adventures as a wine merchant. Such were the vagaries of the Australian marriage market: Robert Jeffray's next daughter, Helen, shortly married the brother of the archetypal imperialist Cecil Rhodes, Ernest. And what could be more romantic than giving birth in a Scottish castle?

Marion appears to have been what her taciturn husband was not. Lord Hawke called her 'a pretty, charming Australian lady', and she followed G. F. devotedly, which meant, as she neared full term of her pregnancy, accompanying him to the shores of Cromarty Firth in Ross-shire. G. F. loved shooting in Scotland: the 1881 census had found him at Dalvina Shooting Cottage in Farr with his Middlesex teammates Alexander Webbe and Sherwin Pearson. Foulis Castle, ancestral seat of the clan Munro, was regularly let to visitors, promising a 5000-acre estate rich in grouse, partridge, woodcock, hares and trout all within half a mile of the railway station.

So it was that George Valentine Jeffray Vernon

first saw the light of day on 19 December 1885; one imagines his father celebrating with a bag of partridges; his godfather was G. F.'s hunting, shooting, fishing and cricketing pal Webbe. The scrapbooks of Foulis Castle contain mementos of the Vernon's tenancy, albeit with imprecise scribblings in the hand of the current clan leader's great aunt. A photograph of G. F. bears the pencilled annotation: *'Australian cricketer.'* A photograph of Marion and George, she buttoned into a dress

The Vernons at Foulis Castle

with an improbably cinched waist, his fat fingers on the handle of a tennis racquet, carries the caption: *'This baby was eventually hanged for murder in South Africa, killed a man with a cricket bat in a fight.'*

*

'This baby', for the time being, seems to have done little to restrict his peripatetic father. Over the next seasons, G. F. played his best and most consistently successful cricket, including his highest score of 160 against Oxford University, and a celebrated partnership with Timothy O'Brien helping Middlesex score 280 in three and a half hours to beat Yorkshire. He took an interest in cricket at Rugby, recommending the appointment as coach of the venerable old pro Tom Emmett to counteract its decline. He indulged a love of alpinism, routinely skipping the last few county fixtures to scale peaks on the continent. Then, in January 1887, G. F. was approached by Major Ben Wardill, secretary of the Melbourne Cricket Club, to recruit another majority amateur team of English cricketers for a tour of the antipodes: his bride, after all, almost made G. F. an honorary Australian.

G. F. VERNON'S AUSTRALIAN TEAM, 1887–8.

RAWLIN M. P. BOWDEN G. F. VERNON SIR T. C. O'BRIEN BEAUMONT
A. E. NEWTON BATES HON. M. B. HAWKE ATTEWELL PEEL
(Captain)
ABEL W. W. READ A. E. STODDART

The enterprise was ill-starred, for also in the works was a tour by a mainly professional English team organised by the trustees of the Sydney Cricket Ground. Nothing much went right. G. F. failed to tempt cricket's chief box office draw, Dr W. G. Grace, with an offer of £2000 plus expenses; his fall back as captain, Hon Martin Bladen Hawke, a twenty-seven-year-old old

Etonian and Cambridge blue descended from the British naval hero, was then doubtful because of the ill-health of his father, the sixth Baronet, til a last-minute acceptance. The twenty-six players of the two teams actually travelled on the same Orient steamer, *Iberia*, mixing freely, even staging a play together: the Sussex amateur C. Aubrey Smith, later Hollywood's go-to Englishman in films like *Lives of a Bengal Lancer*, played the lead in Byron's *Old Soldiers*. But on arrival G. F. injured himself by falling down a companionway, and his team lost its opening match, to New South Wales, by a big margin.

Performances stabilised – from there, in fact, G. F.'s ensemble would not lose again. But its luck never improved. Three weeks before Christmas, Hawke looked up from writing a letter home to see G. F. arm-in-arm with Surrey amateur Walter Read 'in deep consultation'. So instant was his foreboding that when G. F. walked in five minutes later, Hawke said: 'You need not tell me, my father is dead'. Two days later he would be en route home to become the seventh Baronet. A still graver tragedy then befell the team's brilliant professional all-rounder Billy Bates, who during a joint practice session at the MCG on 21 December was struck by a drive from Bill Newnham, an amateur member of the other team, batting in the adjacent net. Loss of the sight of his left eye effectively cost Bates his livelihood. Devastated, he would try cutting his throat on the way home. As stand-in skipper, G. F. probably did a good job maintaining his team's morale. But 'the summer of the two tours' was a financial debacle for its respective backers. 'Probably there never was such a prominent case of folly in connection with cricket,' averred Hawke.

Marion Vernon not only returned to Australia with her husband, but accompanied him the following winter on the first English tour of Ceylon and India, again gathered by G. F., again led by the young buck who had now become Lord Hawke. She and the wife of the amateur George Lawson-Smith were the only women on the trip. British India offered inferior cricket but better hunting and richer hospitality than Australia. To the *Bombay Gazette*, Hawke spoke of 'a trip round India, doing some shooting and having a few games at cricket on our way'. In fact, G. F. had to assume the captaincy when Hawke promptly fell ill, and saw little of the country unrelated to cricket and to killing. 'Almost the only sights I saw in India were the Church and Memorial Wall at Cawnpore and the Taj Mahal,' G. F. would recall, although he liked it well enough to go on a second tour there three years later.

Where, all this time, was young George? There is no mention of him, and a cricket tour that was barely a place for a woman would scarcely have been a place for a child. Based on G. F.'s cricket calendar, not to mention his legal work and field recreations, he must have been a classically distant Victorian paterfamilias – ever more distant, in fact.

*

In July 1893, G. F. embarked aboard the *Austral* for the fledgling gold fields of Coolgardie and Murchison. These were then the world's most alluring, and would in a decade yield more than £10 million of gold. 'Heaps of it!' exclaims the prospector of Nat Gould's *The Miner's Cup* (1896). 'Gold, gold, gold! Pure solid gold! Millions of it!' Miners, diggers, carters and teamsters erected a town 'as if in a night', striking claims with such names as 'Croesus', 'Brilliant Reward' and 'Wealth of Nations'. Among them, as warden, was G. F's old Rugby schoolmate, John Finnerty; also the incorrigible fabulist William Carr-Boyd and Lord Alfred Douglas's brother Percy. G. F. himself enjoyed a pale fame amid the fossickers and financiers. 'Our City Man' in *The British Australasian* described 'the once renowned cricketer' in December 1894 as giving 'a thoroughly coherent and impartial account' of the various mining prospects.

> Mr. Vernon thinks very highly of the Golconda, which was floated here a few weeks back. The Kinsella, he also says is on a good line; whilst Abbott's he has heard very highly spoken of, though he has not investigated it personally. Yalgoo, Mr Vernon is also a believer in, so that shareholders in the Emerald may look forward to their investment with undiminished confidence. Mr Vernon is a fine manly specimen of a type which it would be very well to see multiplied amongst the exploiters of Western Australia. He talks of going back to the Murchison at an early date, and if any one wants trustworthy

advice as to how best to invest his money in what
it is the general opinion will prove hardly second
to Coolgardie as a gold-producer, he could not go
to a better source.

In fact, the Golconda quickly petered out, to
the disillusionment of London shareholders; so
did a nearby mine, Vernon's Pride, which may
have been named for G. F. But why did a London
barrister converge on a gilded fly-speck in the
Australian wilderness? A man only undertakes
such a journey for one reason, and that is money –
which G. F. did not make.

Ironically, Marion's family had gone from
strength to strength: her father Robert was now
on the board of the Australian Pastoral Company,
one of the biggest owners of freehold land in
Queensland. But the 1890s were hungry decades
for those members of Britain's leisure society
without secure fortunes. When they inherited the
Darnley estate, the Blighs would find that it had
been picked clean by his schizophrenic brother
and an improvident younger wife; the Nevills
would be left high and dry by the South American
railway bust. Lord William was chagrined to end

up selling insurance, complaining: 'It is absurd to expect that I should work on the same terms as ordinary agents, as my name and position must be worth something.' Ten years after having been the colonies' suavest bachelor, his lordship served five years in prison for conning another man into signing five promissory notes.

The Vernons, who described themselves in the census as 'living on own means', did not come so conspicuously a cropper, but they acquired no property, and abandoned a picturesque rental in Brompton's Egerton Gardens with as many as five servants for an apartment in a Victorian mansion block in Westminster's Ashley Gardens with only a housekeeper. Young George would not follow his father to Rugby. Young George would not follow his father anywhere.

G. F. Vernon in 1897

*

In July 1897, around the time he last appeared for Middlesex, G. F. afforded Bettesworth the only significant interview of his career. An anecdote stands out, from the game in which he led his Englishmen against New South Wales a decade earlier.

> I remember that in one of the matches in Sydney, Percy McDonnell skied a ball to me when his score was about 112. I saw in a moment that I should have to remain exactly where I was – that is to say near the ropes within a couple of yards of the crowd, who seemed to realise my position almost as soon as I did myself. I have a vivid recollection of their remarks while I was waiting for the ball to drop. It went very high and seemed as if it were never going to come down, and by the time I made the catch my left leg began to shake in a way I did not like at all. However, it all came right in the end.

It is an unusual self-disclosure, accentuating the stress of the instant, and perhaps the peculiar anxiety this incurably restless man experienced when required to stay in the one place – as he was just about to. G. F.'s beloved Marion began suffering the nausea, fatigue, breathlessness and bloating that preluded worsening illness. Lord Hawke described her as having 'bravely faced the terrible disease to which she succumbed'. Aged thirty-eight, Marion died at home in Ashley Gardens on 5 November 1900 of 'exhaustion and collapse' brought about by a 'malignant ovarian tumour', leaving forty-year-old G. F. and fourteen-year-old George – although not, it would seem, together. G. F. soon after was living in lodgings in St James Street, giving his address as the nearby Conservative Club, giving his occupation as 'of independent means'. George can barely have seen his father again.

Why did G. F. join the Colonial Service? Most probably, he needed the money. And, especially to one related by marriage to Cecil Rhodes, Africa seemed to offer the kind of raw adventure and gracious living no longer available at home. James Bryce's influential recent travelogue *Impressions of South Africa* (1899) included such promising vignettes of Rhodesia as:

The first sign that we were close upon Gwelo came from the sight of a number of white men in shirt-sleeves running across a meadow—an unusual sight in South Africa, which presently explained itself as the English inhabitants engaged in a cricket match. Nearly the whole town was either playing or looking on. It was a hot afternoon, but our energetic countrymen were not to be scared by the sun from the pursuit of the national game. They are as much Englishmen in Africa as in England, and, happily for them and for their country, there is no part of the national character that is more useful when transplanted than the fondness for active exercise.

There might even be the gold that had eluded G. F. in Australia, and he opted eventually for the Gold Coast, recently secured by the subduing of the Ashanti, and predicted to be 'one of (if not the) richest gold bearing countries in the world.' In March 1902, Rhodes died, mouthing his famous last words: 'So much done – so much to do.' It was a portentous month for G. F. to embark for a portentous destination: Port Elmina, the continent's oldest European settlement.

But Port Elmina, surrounded by mangroves and reliant on tank water, was also part of the world's worst malarial vector. The disease accounted for nine in every ten deaths in the expatriate community; it did for G. F. As the Empire prepared to celebrate the coronation of Edward VII, he came down with fever; a day into the reign of the new king, he died, aged forty-six.

When old clubmates like Webbe and Pearson convened Middlesex's annual meeting at Charing Cross Hotel soon after, they bowed their heads solemnly for a concluding minute: 'The sad death of Mr G. F. Vernon who for so many years played for the county, was alluded to in very feeling terms, and a unanimous vote of sympathy was passed. This will be forwarded in due course to Mr Vernon's son.' 'In due course' because George Vernon was at sea.

2

'THE SUPERFLUOUS SON'

So the Victorian boy became an Edwardian orphan, and one with proportionally diminished prospects. The Vernons' lifestyle had left little over: his mother's and father's estates would amount to barely £200 between them. Young George passed uneasily into the custody of his aunt Helen and her husband Ernest Rhodes, a retired captain of Royal Engineers, who lived in Aldershot Park with their younger children Georgia, Violet and Francis and no fewer than nine domestic staff – a taste of wealth and comfort, although these were not his. On 15 May 1901, aged fifteen, Vernon, G. V. J. commenced fifteen months as a naval cadet on the training ship *Britannia*, an old three-decker moored at the mouth of the Dart.

The new cadet was essentially bullied and brutalised into line. 'There were many stern, unwritten laws which he had to pick up as best he could, for he was told nothing,' recalled a

HMS Britannia

contemporary. 'The whole system inevitably meant that only fittest survived.' Scurrying along the rigging, wrestling ruleless bouts, running with the beagle pack: these could hardly have suited a rather protected only child, and George left with a chequered progress report committing officers to a quarterly update on his development, 'his character while on *Britannia* only having been fair, he being lazy and lacking in interest in his work.' It was on top of this, as he received his first posting, that George received news of his father's distant death.

There was less rum, sodomy and the lash on *HMS Grafton*, an Edgar-class protected cruiser in the Navy's Pacific Fleet on the west coast of the Americas, based in Esquimault in British Columbia. The fleet's duties were essentially ceremonial – indeed the Royal Navy would abandon the Pacific Station a few years later. A diary of a young *Grafton* officer, Ralph Clayton, contains its share of idle time, on shore and at sea, and duties accented to maintenance of the ship, courses in gunnery and mine-laying, preparation for exams. The *Grafton* was an old, uncomfortable vessel, inadequately ventilated, poorly fitted out, and George's birthday would have found him coaling in the equatorial heat of Acapulco. But Christmas involved a shore picnic of shooting, fishing and swimming, and George became a full midshipman on 30 December 1902. A report a few weeks later indicated 'satisfactory progress.'

Then, on a goodwill trip to San Francisco timed to coincide with the city visit of president Teddy Roosevelt, something went amiss. On 11 May 1903, the *Grafton* crossed the Golden Gate, to be greeted by a twenty-one-gun salute from Fort

Point and Fort Alcatraz, which it reciprocated, and which was followed by a thirteen-gun salute from the *USS New York*. The *Grafton's* band alternated renditions of 'God Save the King' and the 'Star-Spangled Banner'; San Fransiscans were invited to tour the ship between 3pm and 5pm. And perhaps in the general mingling, Midshipman George Vernon went missing. Clayton noted 'a lot about it in the papers' for such an absconding was an unusual occurrence 'although there was a case in the Mediterranean of two Mids deserting'. Vernon had not reappeared when the *Grafton* sailed two days later, so was listed as deserting also.

To where did Vernon vanish in the San Francisco of 1903? It was an exuberant, gaudy city of 350,000, famous for its hospitality, notorious for its Chinatown, with a mayor in Handsome Gene Schmitz who would serve time for graft. Its siren song would have been hard for a sheltered seventeen-year-old Englishman to resist. After a while, too, there was a pressure to remain out of sight – he was, in effect, on the run, although there was benefit that his famous name meant nothing here. All that George would later divulge was that 'influence got my pardon from the Admiralty'. It may have been exerted by Lord Hawke, himself childless but having promised G. F. he would 'look out for George', and whose family name still carried weight in naval circles: *Grafton's* sister ship, in fact, was *HMS Hawke*.

'Withdrawn June 03', reads Vernon's naval personnel file, with a further emendation: next to the heading 'parent or guardian', G. F.'s name has been crossed out for that of his aunt Helen, who by now lived at Binfield Lodge, a large house on landscaped surrounds in Berkshire's Bracknell Forest once owned by William Pitt. It became official on the order of the High Court on 18 November 1904 that Helen had been 'duly elected by the said minor for his use and benefit and until he shall attain the age of 21 years.' But George was now in limbo. The career paths acceptable to one of his class were essentially closed to him: the military was no longer an option; the English common law was more refined and complicated than in his father's day; the civil service was now recruiting by 'open competition'. There was the City, but George exhibited no aptitude for it; there was the church, but most urban diocese were well stocked with clergy after a period of ecclesiastical reform. One imagines family conclaves, also involving G. F.'s friends Webbe and Hawke, about finding some means of settling the boy, who was not to be a boy much longer.

*

It was John Stuart Mill's father James who described Britain's empire as 'a vast system of outdoor relief for the upper classes'; it at least gave George Vernon somewhere to go. Shortly after obtaining his majority, he struck out, like his father, for Africa. 'Influence', he explained, had opened doors for him in Rhodesia, which given his uncle must have seemed like a family heirloom. On the nominal roll of the British South African Police in Salisbury he became number 762 on 5 February 1906.

The South African Police were not everyday constabulary, but the military patrolmen inaugurated by Cecil Rhodes' British South African Company in 1889; rankers had been conspicuous in the Jameson Raid and the Boer War. The force recruited from across the Empire, including many from Australia, so became something of a counterpart to the Foreign Legion in *Beau Geste*. Trooper Vernon outlasted his father at least, spending two years bossing round natives, rounding up Chinese and suppressing the grog trade. But it was an undistinguished sojourn: he received neither promotions nor decorations and was reported for drunkenness on no fewer than five occasions. Securing his 'discharge by purchase' on 11 April 1908, George returned to England.

Still his circle continued believing that the Empire might yet make something of George – or, at least, save them the trouble. Indeed, he was the perfect candidate to become a 'remittance man': a male youth who for whatever reason a family found inconvenient to have at home in England, and to whom they effectively paid a stipend to remain abroad. Some were victims of primogeniture – the legal convention of settling estates on first sons, leaving the rest to scrabble for financial security on a patriarch's death. But for many families, it also offered a solution to criminal conviction, social scandal, illegitimacy, improvidence and other forms of disgrace.

Such aimless wanderers were stock characters of empire, usually the worse for drink. A cheerfully blithe remittance man is the chief protagonist of Robert Louis Stevenson's grand south seas yarn *The Wrecker* (1892); a charmingly dissipated one features in Mark Twain's *Following the Equator* (1897):

> Passengers explained the term to me. They said that dissipated ne'er-do-wells belonging to important families in England and Canada were not cast off by their people while there was any hope of reforming them, but when that last hope perished at last, the ne'er-do-well was sent abroad to get him out of the way. He was shipped off with just enough money in his pocket—no, in the purser's pocket—for the needs of the voyage—and when he reached his destined port he would find a remittance awaiting him there. Not a large one, but just enough to keep him a month. A similar remittance would come monthly thereafter. It was the remittance-man's custom to pay his month's board and lodging straightway—a duty which his landlord did not allow him to forget—then spree away the rest of his money in a single night, then brood and mope and grieve in idleness till the next remittance came. It is a pathetic life.

Canada was the biggest pasture for black sheep: it was near, big and wild, albeit slightly less wild than the American west, its frontier more orderly for government land surveys, homestead regulation and leasing agreements. A man could lose himself there – even a cricketer could. W. G. Grace's cousin Walter Raleigh Gilbert, having struggled to afford to play cricket as an amateur and been caught rifling teammates' pockets in a dressing room at Cheltenham in 1886, ended up seeing out his days there: *Wisden* referred to his 'disappearance' from cricket as involving events of which there was 'no need to speak'. A. N. Hornby's son Jack embarked for Halifax in April 1904 with ambitions to become a heroic 'Hermit of the Arctic' – an expeditionary path that led to his death in the Barren Lands.

George Vernon had lesser aspirations when he embarked on the *Kensington* for Montreal. His destination was Calgary, known as 'the Mecca of the superfluous son' because of the guileless remittance men wandering the streets in garish cowboy rigs that locals had conned them into buying. 'Thither go the young gentlemen from England who cannot, or do not, pass their examinations,' wrote a contemporary observer. 'Or cannot, or will not, sit on a stool in father's office or who have neither the capacity nor the will to make for themselves acceptable careers in the Old Country.' They could at least make good in fiction: dutiful and obedient 'Hon Percy Rapson, late of Eton College, now of Rattlesnake Ranch' was the hero of a string of novels by Robert Leighton; Ralph Connor created the memorable 'Duke', able to 'rope a steer, bunch cattle, play poker or drink whisky to the admiration of his friends and the confusion of his foes.' But George only seems to have developed the last of these faculties.

'Whisky is the curse of the country,' Edward Ffolkes had warned in *Letters of a Young Immigrant in Manitoba* (1883). 'One taste and they say it is like opium – it is impossible to give it up.' George followed heedlessly in the footsteps of one of the frontier's great dandies. Coutts Marjoribanks' decadent excesses had led to his being cut off by his father Lord Sir Dudley Coutts Marjoribanks of Tweedmouth. His good fortune was to have an indulgent older sister, Ishbel, who persuaded her husband the Earl of Aberdeen, Canada's Governor-General, to fix Coutts up with a sizeable allowance and a series of ranches. Coutts furnished one of them, Coldstream, in the Okanagan Valley, with a magnificent ranch house, festooned with seven chimneys and lined with gold Japanese wallpaper. He then scrupulously abjured all agricultural activity, preferring to hunt, shoot, fish and spend – and it was here, probably in the overpriced corduroy trousers, pea jacket and high boots by which the remittance man was usually identified, that George would end up for several months.

It was not a successful graft – none were. George moved on through several ranches, including a cattle farm in Alberta and an orchard in California, slipping into the remittance man's binge-and-starve cycle – magnanimous when money arrived, importunate when it ran out. He dabbled in mining, indulged in rafting, wandered in circles, drank too much, and wound up in Winnipeg, albeit at an unpromising time. Weary of the prodigality of remittance men, the Farm Help Register had begun scribbling at the bottom of its advertisements: 'No Englishmen Need Apply.' George had to take other steps. He joined the Royal Canadian Mounted Rifles, but after three months secured his 'discharge by purchase'. He joined the Permanent Army Medical Corps two days later, but after another three months deserted.

By May 1909, George was back in England, but otherwise lost, having failed to get an education, get married or find a career, and having flunked out of four different uniforms in three different continents. The only person known to have seen him was his father's old friend, Hawke, in what was actually the summer of his lordship's apotheosis, when *Wisden* extolled his influence on cricket as that of an 'absolute master' who had 'always used his power wisely'. On his advice or not, George now had a new destination. On 11 June, he took a second-class passage on the Orient liner *Omrah*. He was bound for Brisbane.

*

Originally, of course, Australia had been a destination of disgrace. But it had also become a land where a man could redeem himself, probably since Caroline Chisholm persuaded Charles Dickens to send Wilkins Micawber to the colonies in *David Copperfield* (1850), a path also followed fruitfully by Abel Magwich in *Great Expectations* (1861). Micawber and Magwich anticipated the journeys undertaken by two of Dickens' more aimless sons, Alfred d'Orsay Tennyson Dickens and Edward Bulwer Lytton Dickens; both managed colonial sheep stations, without ever quite outgrowing their patrimony. Anthony Trollope's son Frederick also managed a sheep station, leading his father to conclude that 'any young man whose courage is high and whose intelligence is not below par...should come out [to Australia].'

Around the turn of the century, this idea of the antipodes as a suitable place for directionless youth was sufficiently proverbial for Oscar Wilde to have it loom over Algernon Moncrieff in *The Importance of Being Earnest* (1895)...

> Cecily: Uncle Jack is sending you to Australia.
>
> Algernon: Australia! I'd sooner die.

Cecily: Well, he said at dinner on Wednesday night, that you would have to choose between this world, the next world, and Australia.

Algernon: Oh, well! the accounts I have received of Australia and the next world are not particularly encouraging.

...and for Hillaire Belloc to spring it on the scapegrace grandson in 'Lord Lundy', in *Cautionary Tales for Children* (1907)...

We had intended you to be
The next Prime Minister but three:
The stocks were sold; the Press was squared:
The Middle Class was quite prepared.
But as it is!...My language fails!
Go out and govern New South Wales!

In Australia, there was some sympathy for the lot of the Englishman so marooned. Some achieved note: his father had sent wild teenager Adam Lindsay Gordon to South Australia, where he became known by his vivid verse in *The Australasian* and *Bell's Life*; exiled to the colonies after an indiscretion in the Artillery, Phil Mowbray had become *The Bulletin's* popular bard of the swag, Scotty the Wrinkler. Others pricked curiosity: enigmatic Jan Digby in Ambrose Pratt's *The Remittance Man* (1907) quickens the pulse of Marion Reay, daughter of a Ballina sugar czar.

Marion Reay meets Jan Digby
in *The Remittance Man*

'What, then, is Mr Jan Digby?'

'A remittance man. He hasn't sixpence in the world, beyond a pittance he receives quarterly through my father's bank from England...He is a rank loafer. He keeps body and soul together by fishing, and he lives in that awful little shanty on the beach...'

Marion experienced a sudden sense of shame to have invited the revelation of such sordid details. 'Let us charge the subject,' she said gravely, with entire frankness. 'I am sorry to have brought it up. Mr Digby may be a rascal, or he may be a gentleman, but in either case we have no right to discuss him to such a point. I feel mean in knowing what you have told me.'

Not only Marion but her younger brother Jack take a shine to Digby, a virile outdoorsmen. When Jack enjoins his father to offer Digby a job as foreman of the local sugar mill, the remittance man takes a principled stand with union workers in a strike, earning the enmity of punitive parliamentarian and love rival Dr Culgin: 'If I had my way, I would re-establish the lash, the pillory and the stocks...I have measured wires with abler men than the remittance man, and I've yet to meet my match. I'll crush him – like that!' But by his personal honour, Digby wins fair Marion, vindicates Jack and regains their father's trust, as the reason for his exile also becomes known.

> 'The letter said that – that you had been brought up as – as Lord ——'s son – but that when he died you cleared out suddenly, and – and afterwards…It came out that – that he had married your mother – after you were born.'
>
> Jan was pale as a sheet. 'He told me so on his death-bed,' he said in deep, low tones.

A writer in *The Age* that same year likewise strove to distinguish remittance wheat from chaff.

> Anyone who has had the pleasure of knowing some of these young bloods knows that in many cases the conventional pictures of them are absurd libels. A number of them certainly have the heavy footed, long striding walk, and wear their trousers well tucked up, as if it were raining heavily in London. A few may even sport an eyeglass and display the languid good humor and the general air of boredom with which the whole class are debited. The newly arrived 'remittance man'—the active, intelligent

fellow who is hot foot after a fortune—feels as much annoyed at the caricature as the son of a Cork man feels at the sight of the long upper lip and the chin whiskers of the stage Irishman.

All the same, wary of the 'idleness of the useless type of young Englishman', the writer saw the road to dissipation as a short one.

When Ethelred—that name will do as well as any other—first came under notice, he walked the Collins-street block with his head in the air, a long, stalking stride, a crooked stick under his arm, his mouth open and his face distorted by the exertion of holding up a tremendous eye-glass, he viewed the evidences of puny Australian industry with supercilious tolerance and talked of 'home' like a patriot. He spent money freely. 'Too early, old chap?' he asked, as he significantly indicated the nearest bar. 'Come on, let's have a small bottle.' Inside the place, he talked like a king and was so gallant and superior that all the bar maids were agreed that he was the son of an Earl at least...

Three weeks later a familiar figure was staggering up Bourke-street with a diminutive, woe-begone looking rough-haired terrier at the end of a cord almost as long as a clothes line.

It was the gallant young Englishman...His once dandy, grey, square-cut suit was soiled and misshapen. His hat was dented, his linen looked as if he had been sleeping in the park, his eyes were blood-shot, and he was unshaven... As his Melbourne acquaintance drew near he stopped and clutched a verandah post. 'I say, old chap,' he said, in the tones of a tragedian, 'do you—hic—want to save a life?...Well, buy me a brandy and soda.'

At least George enjoyed some advantages in heading for Australia. His mother and her family had been Australian; in London, he left his grandfather Robert, chairman of the Australian Pastoral Company; in Brisbane, he would be joining his uncle Alan, manager of Australian Estates & Mortgage, son-in-law of the pastoralist Walter Hays and brother-in-law of the successful barrister Allan Macnaughton. He even had a connection to the Governor of New South Wales, Viscount Chelmsford, who as the Hon Frederic Thesiger John Napier had played with and against his father for Middlesex and the Gentlemen, in addition to being a member of the Inner Temple.

Whatever his prior scrapes, George Vernon was a youth with an entree to Australia's circles of wealth and influence.

So it was that on the morning of 29 July 1909, George descended the gangway of the *Omrah* to meet Alan Jeffray. Jeffray was forty, tall and courtly, the mannerisms and accent he had picked up at Harrow having withstood many subsequent years in Townsville. George Vernon was twenty-four, stocky and still youthful in appearance, and, for the moment at least, probably hopeful.

3

'A MOONLIGHT NIGHT'

About the night of 23 September 1910, everyone on Doondi Station in Queensland's Darling Downs remembered the moon. Shortly to enter its last quarter, it rose into the cloudless sky about 10.40pm, casting a pale glow over the station buildings. A hundred and more years ago, it was commoner to speak of a 'moonlight' than a 'moonlit' night, and this was the phrase that recurred in people's recollections. In the words of the stable boy Edgar Bowman: 'The night was a bright moonlight and I could see a man quite plain.'

Because this light concerned more than atmospherics. The Doondi Station Mystery, as it would become, pivoted on identification. Otherwise the case was more or less circumstantial, impressionistic, and possibly personal – an outcome of the particular dynamics of the half dozen people there that fateful night. It was a ragtag crew. Bowman, a fourteen-year-old 'half-caste', was sharing a bunk bed in the single men's hut

EDGAR BOWMAN.

CHARLES CECIL DREW.

RALPH BURDEKIN.

MRS. BURDEKIN.

with a recently-arrived musterer, Charlie Drew. In a corner room of the pine-slab, iron-roofed station store was the gardener, whiskery sixty-year-old Jack Neil. Asleep in a bedroom attached to the station kitchen was the camp cook Ralph Burdekin, with his housekeeper wife Isabella. And in a bedroom in the main station building, whose window looked out on the fast-flowing Balonne River, was George Vernon.

George, now twenty-four, had been sixteen months in Australia. His progress, as ever, had been chequered. Australian Pastoral Company's Sydney-based general manager Bill Young had first found George a berth on Narine, a small station at Dirranbandi, 120km south of the town of St George. Early in the year, however, there had been an incident involving the theft of whiskey from the camp store, and George had been moved to Doondi about 140km north-east. On the evening in question, in fact, George was nominally in charge. Manager Arthur Higginson had left in early afternoon — he was also responsible for managing Gulnarber, on the other side of the Balonne — and was not to return until the next day.

These were not the only people in the vicinity. About 275 metres from the station buildings, on the Balonne's east bank, were four shearers, Alexander Sutherland, Bill McCoy, Henry Berry and Mark Lyons, who had camped overnight on their progress from St George to Yamburgen. About 12km away, camping at Donnelly's Well, was station hand Henry Richardson; at distances of 7km and 25km were camps of Chinese ring-barkers, contracted to Bill Young by Ah Chow. Also part of Ah Chow's duties was provisioning the camp store, most recently a week earlier. This, it would be recounted, had become a source of mild tension.

Life on Doondi was hard. The weather was hot. The flies were relentless. The diet of damper and billy tea was poor, and everyone suffered Barcoo Rot – the slow healing of sores, effectively from malnourishment. George had brought with him to Doondi a bag with cricket bat, boots, pads, and gloves, but nobody else played, despite the presence on the station verandah of two other bats of unknown provenance. Just about the only distraction or comfort on offer was whisky.

Higginson rationed it by the nip (about 30ml) – it served almost as a kind of currency, like the naval tot of rum. Tired? Bored? Sociable? Sick? A nip was the answer. So Ah Chow's delivery on 16 September of no fewer than seventeen cases of Dawson's, each containing a dozen bottles, had not gone unnoticed. Richardson would recall George Vernon approaching him confidentially in the horse yard soon after the unloading. 'The Chinaman unloaded the rations in a room today,' George had said, pointing to the store. 'There is a lot of grog with it. Twenty cases of whisky and sure as the world it will be raided. If so, I will be blamed for it. I raided the chinaman's store at Narine for grog and it's a wonder I didn't get three months.' Richardson was surprised by George's candour; further surprised when the conversation turned to Neil. Richardson had found Neil 'a quiet, inoffensive old chap'; George referred to him angrily as 'an old crawler'.

George repeated similar sentiments that 23 September morning on riding out at daybreak with Drew. Drew had been instructed by Higginson to repair a fence 10km away; George brought his rifle to shoot pigs. They made conversation about the characters on the station, to whom Drew was new, including the sixty-year-old gardener. 'What kind of a fellow is old Jack Neil?' Drew asked. 'I think he is an old informer,' George replied savagely. 'He used to work for a man named Rutledge and I think he was much in his confidence. He is one of those old buggers that when he gets drunk he wants to make a speech.' Drew was puzzled by the vehemence of the comment – like Richardson, he had found the old man perfectly benign. But as a kind of bonding ritual, Drew offered his companion a nip from the whisky flask he was carrying. George shook his head. 'I'll have it in the evening,' he said. Drew returned to the homestead, George continued shooting until his ammunition was exhausted.

As George returned about 5.30pm, he encountered the shearer Berry, walking away from the station to the riverbank where the visitors had deposited their swags. They struck up a halting conversation. Where was Berry going? To Yamburgan. What was George doing? He had been pig shooting. What was up? 'A horse kicked me the other day,' George complained, pointing to a mark on his chin. Eventually he invited the shearer for a drink, but Berry said that his mates were waiting, so George continued to the cart shed, tied his horse, fed his dog, bumped again into Drew. 'What about that present you were going to make me this morning?' said George.

Drew confessed he had forgotten about it, and invited George to his room for a nip.

By now, night was falling. Neil looked in to say hello. Drew offered him a nip also. 'Thank you,' Neil replied. 'But I never drink at night.' Again, there seemed something in the air. When the old man withdrew and Drew commented on his abstemiousness, George commented acidly: 'Oh fuck him. You did not want to offer that old bugger any. He would not offer you any. He has always got some up in his own room.' A desultory conversation continued for half an hour until, just before 7pm, George said he should be going. Isabella served him some of Ralph's hash in the dining room, before he retired to his adjacent bedroom. Just as Drew and Bowman were turning in around 9pm, Neil briefly popped his head in.

'Will I wake you early to get the horses, Edgar?' he asked. 'Not too early,' stipulated Bowman. The last acetylene lamps were extinguished; only the moonlight remained.

*

The Maranoa district had first been traversed by the New South Wales surveyor-general Sir Thomas Mitchell; the location of the town of St George commemorates his 1846 river crossing. The explorer praised the Balonne's 'splendid reaches', thought it 'as fine a looking river as I have seen in the colony, excepting only the Murray.' It sounded enticing to the squatter-settlers who spilled into the area in his wake such as Charles Brown Fisher, who accumulated two million acres. Covering about 400 square kilometres, Doondi, pronounced Doon-Die, was one of his medium-sized stations, albeit well-appointed; the station house was set off by pretty flower beds and a productive vegetable garden; its posts were ornamented with two immense heads of Balonne cod. A visitor in the late 1880s was Constance Ellis, father of the later biographer of Macquarie and Macarthur, whose husband was a bookkeeper on Narine. 'In those days,' she recalled in her lively memoir *I Seek Adventure*, 'a man could spend a week on a station just as a visitor, and get his tucker bags filled when he left and possibly a new shirt or boots or even moleskins given to him. They were great times for the swaggies.'

The Balonne, as seen by Major Mitchell

Thanks to a looming depression, however, these were even then becoming less opportune times for owners. When Fisher overextended, he sold up for a million pounds to APC, a specially-constructed syndicate. This was growing reality of Australia's rural economy. The average pastoral worker of the late nineteenth and early twentieth century was not a bold land baron or even a hardy smallholder; he was the employee of an absentee corporate owner. In a quarter of a century on the board of APC, George's London-based grandfather Robert Jeffray visited Australia twice, without making it to the Maranoa. Mind you, even the member for Balonne, Ted Land, a hotelier in Cunnumulla who served in ten parliaments, confined himself to a single annual visit to St George.

It was harsh country. Sheep were menaced by predators and flystrike. Rabbit before myxomatosis and prickly pear before cactoblastis were tides to hold back. Then there was head office, where Bill Young, in his spectacles and visor, kept a gimlet eye on expenses: a dawn-to-dark shift was known on APC stations as 'a Billy Young day'.

Still, it worked. By 1910, the Maranoa was again prospering, home to 2.8 million of Queensland's 20 million sheep. Though containing fewer than 1000 people, St George was a tidy little town, with a hospital, a police barracks, half a dozen hotels and a number of banks.

More than 500km from Brisbane, the Maranoa counted as remote. St George was beyond the reach of electricity and locomotives; the Cobb & Co stagecoach remained the main link to the world beyond. Gulnarber had a telephone but not Doondi; the telegraph in St George's post office had not long displaced the carrier pigeon as the principal form of communication. In that sense, it was a good place to send a 'young blood' to obtain 'colonial experience', and many such youthful Englishmen had preceded George Vernon. One of them had with his fellow jackaroos composed a tune that was a standard of the Australian stockmen's songbook. C. E. Bowler, later a successful surveyor, set 'The Stockman's Last Bed' to the melody of Charles Dibdin's 'East Whistle'.

> Whether stockman or not, for one moment give ear,
> Poor Jack he is dead, and no more shall we hear
> The crack of his whip, or his horse's sling trot,
> His clear 'go-ahead' or his jingling quart-pot.
>
> For he lies where the wattles their sweet fragrance
> shed,
> And tall gum-trees shadow the stockman's last bed.

When drafting one day, down came his good horse.
'Alas!' cried poor Jack, 'I have run my last course
And never again shall my saddle regain,
Or fleetly bound over the wide-spreading plain.

'Oh! bury me where wattles their sweet fragrance
    shed,
And tall gum-tree shadow the stockman's last bed.'

His whip is now silent, his dogs they now mourn,
His horse stands awaiting his master's return.
Unheeded, uncared for, neglected he died,
Save Australia's dark children none knows where
    he's laid.

Then stockmen, if ever on some future day
While following a mob you should happen to stray –
Think of the spot where poor Jack he is laid
Far, far from the home where in childhood he
    played,
And tread lightly where wattles their sweet
    fragrance shed,
And tall gum-tree shadow the stockman's last bed.

'Poor Jack, he is dead.' One wonders whether
George Vernon ever sang it.

*

It was nearing midnight when the alarm was raised.
Isabella was awoken in the Burdekins' bedroom by

muffled cries of 'someone in distress', and roused her husband, who went to the window and raised the blind. The window was not glass but lattice, with some of the wooden slats missing, and offered a partial view of the store building twenty-five metres away. Ralph Burdekin would swear that he saw the back of a white-clad figure in Neil's room: 'The man had his hands above his head and a light in his hand, his hands were together. I saw the light applied by that man to the valance hanging down from the top of the bed near part of bed the light being applied that part of bed burst into flames and lighted up room.' The man then walked out of view 'clutching something close to his left side'.

Much would later be made of the fact that the Burdekins did not go directly to Neil's room but sought first to rouse Drew and Bowman in the single men's hut seventy metres away, and that they did not sprint ('We walked very quickly, we did not run'). At this stage, however, there was no reason to suspect anything but a fire, and that would need the attention of more than one man. Drew and Bowman dressed hastily and equipped themselves for a blaze: Drew pulled on his trousers, grabbed a

DOONDI STATION.

On the Balonne River, St. George District, where the alleged murder took place. It is owned by the Australian Pastoral Company—a huge agglomeration of absentees—which owns many runs in this and other districts. The figure 1 in the drawing marks the window of the cook's room, at the end of the kitchen, from which the cook says he watched what happened in the room in the store through the window. Fig 2. Fig. 3 is the gate through which the same witness alleges he saw a man pass on his way back to the house (Fig 4) after coming out of Neil's room.

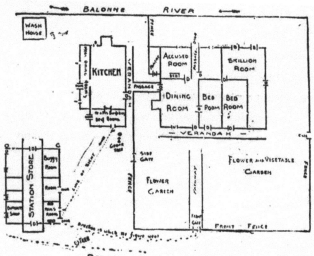

whip handle; Bowman donned his boots and cap, and took a pick; they drew buckets of tank water.

When they got there, the earlier flames had mostly given way to thick smoke. The dry-grass in the bed tick was smouldering, the pine wall and calico ceiling were scorched; they poured out their pails to prevent the fire flaring, then fetched more. Only on striking a match did the group make Neil out clearly: in his shirt and drawers, the gardener was kneeling at the foot of his bed, between two crumpled blankets, groaning as he cradled his freshly bloodied head. 'What's the matter, Jack?' said Drew. 'What has happened?'

'I don't know,' replied Neil groggily.

'Who did this?' Drew continued.

Neil simply repeated: 'I don't know.'

'Have you had any drink?' the musterer asked.

'No,' said Neil. 'Not a drop.'

As Drew helped Neil to his feet, and Ralph Burdekin sat him on the end of the bed, Isabella standing outside caught a glimpse of George Vernon, in an overcoat over pale pyjamas and grey socks, approaching from the gate near the kitchen. Seeing the men, he paused, stopped at the open door, and turned to Burdekin. 'Why did you not call me before?' he asked. 'Call you?' returned Burdekin.

Yet it was not a completely misplaced question. After all, Burdekin and other station occupants would agree that George Vernon was the senior person on Doondi in Higginson's absence. The simple answer is that Burdekin recognised his nominal boss as the likeliest perpetrator; he would describe George as 'excited', his eyes 'bulging out of his head'. He wasn't alone. Drew, on the basis of his earlier conversation with George about Neil, would say that he 'immediately suspected Vernon'; like the cook, he claimed to have seen a fresh patch of blood on the back of the Englishman's hand.

Drew took the Englishman's arm and drew him into the room. 'There's been some dirty work done here,' he said. 'Do you know anything about this?'

'No,' George insisted – and continued, in a way, to assert his rank and birth. 'There are four men camped down on the river,' he said. 'I know one of them. One of them may have run amok. Will we go down and see if they are all there?'

It was a question rather than an order, but Drew acquiesced. 'Yes all right,' he said. 'You had better get your rifle.'

'Some of us had better remain here and look after old Jack,' offered Burdekin.

'No,' said George. 'Let us all go down.' So Drew, Bowman and the Burdekins left behind a badly injured man because an Englishman had told them to. Colonial deference ran deep.

The evening was clear. 'It was a moonlight night when this conversation took place,' Isabella recalled. 'It was a bright moonlight night,' recalled McCoy, 'and I saw the party coming towards the camp when they were some distance away.' He sat up quickly as the visitors approached: 'Good heavens, what's this?'

George responded with his own question: 'Did anybody see anything?'

The shearers looked at each other: nobody had seen a thing. 'Would you mind coming up please?' Ralph Burdekin asked. 'Something terrible has happened. The old gardener is knocked out and someone set fire to the place.'

'Does anybody know surgical work?' George added. Sutherland, oldest of the group, a tall man known inevitably as 'Tiny', said no, but that he would do the best he could.

ALEX. SUTHERLAND.

WILLIAM McCOY.

It was now that George's behaviour began to take curious turns. As they headed back towards the station, McCoy asked George if he had a theory as to the assailant, and was taken aback by the response: 'I don't know as he was not very well liked in these parts. He was a bloody old crawler.' It was the first of a string of comments that non-plussed almost everyone.

When they arrived, Sutherland led the way into the room with a lit match, then was brought a candle. The light revealed extensive cuts on Neil's face; the old man murmured that his wrist was broken also. George turned unbidden to Isabella. 'This is a terrible thing that has happened, Mrs Burdekin,' he said. 'You know Jack is not a very popular man and he has got a lot of enemies. No-one dislikes him more than I do, although I would not hurt him.'

After Isabella and her husband retreated to the kitchen to light the stove and warm the water for the strips of calico that would have to serve as bandages, other dismissive remarks tripped from George's tongue: 'The old man was not well liked generally and I do not care for him'; 'We can do nothing til daylight'; 'It might be a black fellow or a Chinaman's work'; 'I am not a rich man but I not mind betting a fiver that they'll never get the man who did this.' When Sutherland suggested that the police be informed, George even retorted: 'Oh bugger the police, they can't do anything in the matter...In South Africa when I was a policeman there we used to tie up the wounds and let them go or send them down to the hospitals and they would be all right in a couple of days.' Drew also noticed that the blood he had seen on George's hand was now gone.

Some behaviours were downright baffling. As Sutherland dressed Neil's headwound, the old man was heard to say that he thought he had been hit with a cricket bat. 'There's not a bat between St George and Dirranbandi!' George scoffed. Except it was known that the station had at least two, while George himself owned a third.

Finally, matters grew murky. When Sutherland asked if any spirits could be found on the station for Neil, George's ears pricked. 'There is whisky in the store but it belongs to a Chinaman,' he said. 'The boss is away and I do not like to get it without permission.' Sutherland told him to get it. 'This man is very low,' the shearer said of Neil.

'Do you think the Chinaman will say anything if we take a bottle of whisky?' George wondered aloud.

'No,' answered Drew. 'Not if it is for old Jack.'

'Will you bear witness that I take it?' asked George. Drew agreed, and they began to walk round the front of the store. But at the front of the butcher shop, the musterer would testify, George let something slip in a near whisper: 'The old bugger caught me taking this whisky and I knocked him on the head. I did not mean to hit him so hard.'

Drew claimed to have been so shocked he made no reply: 'I was too surprised to say anything.' But he also noticed that when they got to the store window there was evidence of prior entry: there was a barrel beneath the sill, and a wire securing the shutter was already loose. 'Mind you bear witness that I took the whisky,' said George as he extracted a bottle from an already open case. Drew nodded.

The whisky seemed to make things worse. When Sutherland held a pannikin of the liquor to Neil's lips, the gardener vomited some black blood. 'That is the end of the old man,' commented McCoy. 'Haemorrhage has set in.' The remark seemed to shake George. 'Don't say that,' he insisted. Then when Sutherland put the bottle down, George suggested that those in the room should have a drink also.

'We ought not to drink it,' said Drew. 'The Chinaman might think we took it for ourselves instead of Neil.' But the motion, as it were, was carried. Each of George, McCoy, Berry, Sutherland,

Lyons and finally Drew took a nip from an enamelled mug, draining the bottle; Bowman, judged too young to join them, looked on.

By now, George's residual authority had dwindled. Sutherland noted that every time he was addressed, George 'looked away and would not look anyone in the face'. When Sutherland suggested sending someone on the station's night horse into the horse paddock to find mounts for a gallop to St George, Lyons believed that George appeared 'not too willing to do so.'

'It's no use you looking,' George said. 'You'll never find them in the dark. The paddock is too scrubby.'

'I'll get the horses,' McCoy offered. 'I'm not afraid.'

George was peeved. 'If you think I have any fear ,' he responded sharply, 'come into my room and I will show you my medals.'

But perhaps sensing the tension, he went with Bowman to retrieve the night horse, which McCoy saddled then rode off in the direction of the horse paddock. As he vanished into the night, George turned to Drew. 'You are a Doondi man,' he said. 'Never mind about the others. Come up to my room and have a drink.'

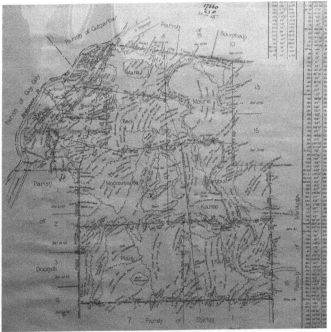

Doondi Map, station in the north-west corner

When Drew told him to bring the whisky over instead, George consented, returning with his own private bottle. It acted like a honey pot. The men gathered on the verandah, taking nips in turn. George started quarrelling with Berry, accusing the shearer of 'following me all night.' He threw off his overcoat and shaped up as if to fight. As Berry backed off, Drew stepped in, and order was restored.

When he returned from brewing tea in the kitchen, however, Ralph Burdekin was shocked to find the men drinking.

'Have a drink,' offered George.

Burdekin grabbed the bottle. 'I'll take charge of this,' he said. 'This is a nice state of affairs. You are the responsible person here and you know how things are over in Neil's room'.

George ignored him. The bottle was almost empty anyway. 'What about another drink?' he asked the group. 'I'll get another bottle from the Chinaman's store. We might as well have it as them.'

As George mooched off to fetch more Dawson's, Burdekin looked in on the failing Neil. 'Poor old man,' he muttered under his breath.

'Is that you, cook?' asked Neil. 'That's me, Jack,' said Burdekin.

'Did you not hear me calling you?' the gardener said weakly.

'No, Jack,' Burdekin replied. 'I'm sorry.' A man was dying, and there was nothing to be done.

*

The night was degenerating. McCoy returned from the horse paddock with several horses, none of which proved amenable to riding, necessitating another excursion. Later accounts would be confused, thanks partly to nobody on the station consulting a watch, partly to the men's worsening intoxication. Nobody drank more than George. As Lyons would say: 'From what I noticed that night the accused seemed to be fond of whisky.' No fewer than six bottles would eventually be found missing from the broken case of Dawson's. Lyons and Sutherland both had flasks as well.

A critical disagreement would emerge around what Neil said. Some, such as Berry, recalled that he could shed no light on his assailant.

> I said to Neil: 'Who done it?'
> He said: 'I don't know.'
> I said: 'Was it a Chinaman or a white man?'
> He said: 'It was a white man.'

Others, like Sutherland, in an exchange corroborated by McCoy, would allege that Neil had specifically fingered George.

> I went into the room and spoke to deceased in the presence and hearing of accused and McCoy.
>
> I said: 'How was it done?' referring to the injuries.
>
> He said: 'It was done with a bat.'
>
> I said: 'Did you have a row with anybody?' He said: 'No.'
>
> I said: 'Who hit you with the bat?' And deceased said: 'He [George] did.'

The only man to keep an entirely clear head, it would appear, was Ralph Burdekin. Though unable to obtain an explicit identification from Neil, he was confounded by George's insouciance, including his aversion to seeking the police. 'What's the point of making a fucking fuss?' George drawled at one point. 'This sort of thing does not happen every night.' Burdekin was appalled: 'My God, it would not want to.' Well in his cups by this stage, George said he would grab an hour's sleep, then ride off to find Higginson. But when

Burdekin went to rouse him, George rolled over and went back to sleep. The cook was then careful to lock the door to Neil's room, so there could be no tampering with its contents.

It would be Drew and Bowman who saddled the horses McCoy had brought in, and who embarked on the two-hour ride north at about 4am. But soon after they disappeared, it grew apparent that Neil might die without medical treatment, so it was decided to convey him to St George Hospital in the station sulky. Complaining of the cold, Neil was dressed, wrapped in a rug, and propped up between Sutherland and Lyons as they took the reins. Dawn was breaking as they embarked in the advance party's wake. It would have been an excruciating progress for a badly injured man over uneven, tussocky ground. 'He appeared to suffer all the way up,' Sutherland recalled, 'and was getting weaker all the time.'

Around 8.30am, about three miles from St George, the party encountered Drew, Bowman and Constable Thomas Cullen coming back the same way. The policeman found Neil lapsing in and out of consciousness. 'What is up, Jack?' asked Cullen.

'Someone hit me with a bat,' Neil replied.

'How do you feel?'

'Pretty bad.' 'Who did it?'

'I don't know,' Neil said, almost inaudibly. 'Have we much further to go?'

The party detoured towards the St George home of Henry Elliott, the local doctor, who found Neil in 'a very collapsed condition and heavy stupor'. Beneath the rudimentary dressings, the man's head was swollen, his eyelids contused; his temples were a mess of wounds, depressions and lacerations; the bone was laid bare on the left side of his forehead. Elliott shepherded the party to the town's little hospital, although he could do little more than bathe and stitch the wounds. Cullen returned to the station to advise his boss, Sergeant Robert Dyer.

St. George Hospital 1906

On Doondi, the day was making a slow start. Isabella Burdekin was too upset to leave her bed; Ralph Burdekin rose to light the stove. Emerging about 9.30am, George lurched into the kitchen, where he declined Burdekin's offer of breakfast.

'What time did Neil leave?' he asked.

'About daylight,' said Burdekin.

'Did Jack say anything? Or recollect anything?'

Burdekin did not reply. He had noticed blood on the inside top portion of George's ears; the blood, he would recall, looked fresh.

Feeling uncomfortable, George went outside, where he encountered Richardson arriving from his overnight camp. To the station hand he appeared 'excited and nervous'; Richardson also noticed spatters of blood on the young Englishman.

'There has been hell to pay since last night,' said George. 'Old Jack has had his bloody brains bashed out.'

'Good God,' gasped Richardson. 'Is Jack dead?'

'No,' George answered. 'Fucking near it.'

George told Richardson that Neil was in hospital, and that he had a theory about the perpetrator: 'It was that Chinaman's whisky. I think Jack and the Chinaman must have been drinking and had a row and after Jack had gone to bed, the Chinaman came back and got to him… You know Jack is not very popular here.'

In Richardson's company, George returned to the kitchen, where Burdekin had been joined by McCoy. To the room he now elaborated his theory. 'It appears to me the work of a black negro or a Chinaman,' George stated. 'I don't profess to be Sherlock Holmes but if I was looking for a perpetrator I would search the Chinese camp.'

Burdekin had had enough. For the first time, he divulged to George that he had caught sight of the killer. 'The man I saw leave Neil's room was dressed in white,' said the cook. George's head dropped. He withdrew silently.

Nobody seems to have directly accused him of the murder that morning, but George's garrulity testifies to his feeling of being suspected. He asked McCoy to join him for a drink – McCoy declined. He asked Isabella Burdekin if she could see Neil's room through her window – she confirmed she could. He suggested to Ralph Burdekin fetching his colt and going in search of Higginson – the cook observed that it would be futile as the boss would already be on his way back. He even agreed to milk some cows in the yard, which was usually Neil's job – they yielded no milk. Others were uneasy too. 'There is meat in the butcher shop that needs putting in the cask,' said Burdekin. But when George wanted Burdekin to come with him, the cook said no. 'I was afraid,' he would explain. He had already quietly secreted George's rifle. When George asked after his 'popgun', Burdekin replied: 'It's all right. I will look after it.' Throughout, he kept drinking, until, at last, he passed out in the dining room.

This was the scene that awaited Higginson on his arrival at noon: the suspect in an assault asleep on a couch, agitated employees explaining that the victim had been despatched and the police been sent for. Higginson was only thirty, but had managed the station for five years and been on it for nine. He had hired most of his men personally, including Burdekin six months earlier. He had found him indifferent as a cook and eccentric as a man but accepted his version of events without difficulty. He realised, shaking George, that the man was 'not sober', but docile at least: 'I had a lot of trouble in waking him. He could stand up. He was drunk. I would not say dead drunk...I told him to go into his own room and stay there. He went into room as ordered.' George was still there when Cullen arrived, after a three-hour ride from town, at 2pm.

A. B. HIGGINSON.
(Manager of Doondi).

Cullen was young: he had turned twenty-four the previous day. St George was his first posting. He had certainly never seen a murder scene, as Burdekin now showed him. The constable sized up the damaged walls, the burned valance, the bloodied grey blanket, and itemised the gardener's few possessions: two pairs of underpants, a broken umbrella, an old mouth organ. A portmanteau beneath the bed, unlocked but undisturbed, contained the unexpectedly large sum of £20 3s 4d: robbery could therefore be excluded as a motivation for the attack. After talking to Burdekin and to Higginson he moved quickly – so quickly it would become an issue – in taking George into custody.

Even at the time it was awkward. When Cullen knocked at George's bedroom there was no answer, and Higginson was needed to unlock the door. George was lying on the bed, dressed, but apparently 'under the influence of drink'.

'Hello,' said Cullen. 'Having a rest?'

'I am waiting to see what you do,' George replied.

'What do you mean?' Cullen asked, but George silently closed his eyes and rolled over. Studying the room, the constable noticed the handle of a bat protruding from a leather cricket bag. He pulled it out. There were 'very distinct' and 'fresh' blood stains on the back and corner. 'Is this your bat?' he asked.

'Yes,' said George curtly. 'What about it?'

Cullen took possession of the bat, the bag and its contents as exhibits. He saw boots and boot stretchers, a saddle pouch full of cartridges, and a towel and pyjamas that appeared bloodstained.

'Were you drinking last night?' he asked casually.

'I had a few with old Jack,' George replied.

'What time did you leave him?'

'About 9pm.'

'How was Neil when you left him?'

'He appeared all right.'

'Neil was taken to hospital today in a very bad state,' Cullen stated, cutting to the chase. 'I now arrest you for assaulting him and causing grievous bodily harm, and warn you that anything you say shall be taken as evidence against you.' When there came neither reply nor stir, the constable put his hand on George's shoulder and said: 'Come on with me.'

'What do you want?' said George.

'I want you to come to St George with me.'

When George continued to make 'no effort to come', Cullen picked him up and dragged him bodily into the dining room, at which point the arrestee slumped on a stretcher. 'Wait 'til I get my coat,' George said at last, but still seemed inert.

Cullen fetched the coat from bedroom, draped it on George's shoulders and repeated: 'Come with me.'

Again George made no move, so Cullen again picked him up beneath the shoulders and commenced dragging him out. Finally, on the verandah, George started to walk unassisted. He stepped down and moved towards the sulky where Higginson stood with Richardson.

'What is wrong, Arthur?' George asked his boss plaintively. 'What does all this mean?'

'I don't know,' said Higginson noncommittally. But he did.

4

'HE'LL SWING FOR IT ALL RIGHT'

As he sobered up on the three-hour sulky ride, George remained silent. He was still wearing the same clothes as the night before – when he was searched at the police lock-up, a bloody handkerchief was found in his left-hand coat pocket and added to the evidence already boxed. But he had not been idle. From St George, both he and Higginson wired Jeffray; George, improbably, also wired his father's old cricket colleague, the Governor of New South Wales. The messages do not survive but from the text of a short letter he sent his uncle the next day, George had clearly been mulling potential alibis and defences.

> Dear Alan,
> You will have got my wire yesterday, also Higginson's: I must leave things in your hands. Please get someone to defend me, and come up yourself if you can. As I was uncertain if you were in Brisbane or not I also wired to Lord Chelmsford, who has wired to Forrest. I am

innocent,
Yours ever, George

Can account for bloodstains on clothing found in room also on bat produced in evidence against me, saw Neil at about 9pm when he gave me meat for dog: another man was present had one drink with other man: declining to make statement until solicitor arrives: deny assault.
George Vernon

The case was indeed still one of the assault, and the police hovered around Neil's bedside in the hope of further information. Whatever he had said to whomever on the station, Neil had given Cullen nothing. Cullen had put George to him as the attacker; Neil had responded: 'I don't know what he would do it for...Leave it for a few days.' Then, after a few more questions, Neil had lapsed into unconsciousness. Cullen's boss Sergeant Robert Dyer asked Elliott if there was any chance police could obtain what was called a 'dying declaration'; Elliott said he would need a day or two to tell. Neil did not have that long. He died, as Constable Arthur Daniels reported to Dyer, at midnight on 26 September without uttering another word. The doctor informed Higginson as the station manager passed through on the way back from nearby Whyenbah station; Higginson carried the news on to Doondi.

With Daniels standing by, Elliott determined at the post mortem that the cause of death was ecchymosis – 'shock and exhaustion' from the after effects of a 'blunt instrument and considerable force.' This

DR. ELLIOTT.

blunt instrument, he would agree, could be George's cricket bat. But the crime, Dyer informed Inspector Charles Savage in Roma, was now a murder without a witness.

Or was there one? After all, Ralph Burdekin claimed to have seen a white-clad figure in the act of igniting Neil's valance. Over the next few days, his view as to the identity of that figure fluctuated. He strongly believed George Vernon to be the killer; but whether George Vernon was the white-clad figure was another matter. After noon on

27 September, even as Neil was being buried in St George, Doondi received a visit from Bill Young's local inspector Thomas Brown, normally based at either of APC's bigger Maranoa stations, Noondoo or Gulnarber. 'I suppose you know old Neil is dead,' said Brown, sitting down in the kitchen with the Burdekins.

'Yes,' confirmed Ralph Burdekin. 'The boss told us when he returned from Whyenbah this morning.' He laughed: 'They have got the right man too.'

'I believe your wife heard him screaming out,' said Brown.

'No,' said Burdekin. 'My wife heard a noise and woke me.' He offered to reenact the scene, and led Brown into the bedroom: he explained that he had risen from bed, raised the blind, and seen a light in Neil's room, whereupon a man had walked out in the direction of the garden gate. Burdekin recalled his remark to Isabella: 'This is some of Vernon's work.' He turned to her for confirmation: 'Didn't I, missus?'

Brown noted Isabella's reaction. 'Oh no,' she said tearily. 'Hold your tongue.'

Pulling the blind to one side and gesturing towards Neil's room, Ralph ploughed on. 'You can see I could see into the room all right. I did not know what to do. I stood for a bit. My wife was screaming and we did not know the minute he was coming to us. We then went down to the men's hut and got them to put the fire out.' He described how George materialised at Neil's room when the fire was extinguished and asked ingenuously: 'Why did you not call me?' He recalled replying: 'Call you?' Isabella was now weeping. 'No, don't,' she protested.

Brown asked whether there had been drinking on the station. Only afterwards, Burdekin insisted, when the bottle had been obtained for Neil: 'Some of the men said we'd better have a drink too. They finished the bottle, and you know what men are;

T. BROWN.
(Witness).

they got at it. I heard them fumbling round and knocking things down on the verandah. I went and took it from them, and told them they ought to be ashamed of themselves.'

'This is different to the story we heard at Noondoo,' Brown commented. 'We heard you had actually recognised Vernon, striking matches and setting fire to the bed, saw him go into the house and he was then covered in blood.'

'No,' said Burdekin. 'I saw a man who looked like him, dressed in white, going across the yard...Everything points to him.' He concluded confidently: 'It was him all right. He had a dark patch on his bat that looked like blood...He'll swing for it all right.'

*

Nine am the next day saw the first step in that direction, when Cullen approached George in the police yard at St George. 'Neil died at 12 o'clock on Monday night at the hospital,' said the constable. 'I now charge you with the wilful murder of one John Neil at Doondi station on 23rd September, 1910, and anything you now say shall be taken as evidence against you.' George said: 'Yes.' The Police Court placed him on remand for the next eight days. The attack finally attracted press attention: reporting developments, St George's *Balonne*

Beacon, [which] commented on the disturbance of 'the usual quietude of our town'. Neil was 'well and favourably known locally, and was generally regarded as a good, kindly dispositioned old man'; Vernon, a 'recent arrival in Queensland from Great Britain' was 'reported to be well educated and very well-connected.'

For the police, such a charge of murder, with a sympathetic victim and a well-to-do assailant, hugely raised the stakes. Could a local station cope? Because law enforcement in rural Queensland was only partly about crime; the local constabulary was an all-purpose bureaucracy with a constantly widening remit. Police were expected to check drovers' waybills, inspect brands, man border crossings, check on slaughter houses, factories, breweries and nursing homes; they had to chase truant children, admit indigent children to institutions, issue rail passes to the destitute, distribute old age pensions, witness post mortems, arrange pauper burials; they had to gather statistics on the cultivation of sugar cane and production of sugar, and issue permits to trappers while also protecting native birds, wombats, possums and koalas. 'As a "handy man" of his country he [the policeman] occupies a unique position,' said a contemporary observer. 'Almost the only fault he has is that he is too willing to take a heavy burden on his back and do work that should fall to others.'

Despite ever-broadening responsibilities, the force was chronically under resourced and underpaid. Police commissioner William Cahill, a former member of the Royal Irish Constabulary, had improved some working conditions: a constable no longer had to pay for his own uniform and could expect a pension on retirement. But the force was infamous for the rank of Acting Sergeant, whereby a man was promoted to the responsibilities of the role without the remuneration. No fewer that 150 of Queensland's thousand policemen were Acting Sergeants, some having held the rank for more than twenty years. To put it plainly, the police was not an employer of choice for the capable and ambitious, and its reputation had hardly recovered from the censure of a Royal Commission for failures to solve a string of heinous late Victorian killings. Bumbling investigation of the so-called Gatton horror – an 1898 family annihilation on a farm at Blackfellow's Creek 100km west of Brisbane – had been held up as particularly indicative of 'a rotten system of policing'.

Commissioner William Cahill

The force's deficiencies would manifest at several stages in the investigation at Doondi – not least in the careless handling of evidence that Cullen had collected from George's room, which was heavily manhandled and roughly strapped aboard a Cobb & Co coach for its three-day journey to Brisbane. Cullen, in his haste to bring the suspect in, had also failed to lock George's bedroom and secure the crime scene. Doondi was a regular stop for stage coaches, to water their horses and rest their passengers – some of the latter, having heard about the bloody crime, took to nosing around the station, peering in on this and that, despite Ralph Burdekin's efforts to shoo them away.

Conscious of the limitations of the outpost at St George, Savage directed reinforcements from Roma and Mungindi. Over the course of three days, Acting Sergeant John McGuire, Senior Constable Denis Quinlan and Senior Sergeant Mathias Daley arrived in St George after coach journeys of several days. They were typical uniformed police of their time: minimally educated, former labourers, Roman Catholics. McGuire, who with Quinlan was sent on to Doondi to reconnoitre the station, had recently been fined £10 for being 'unfit to perform his duty, in consequence of being temporarily insane from excessive use of alcohol'.

Stopping overnight in St George, Daley interviewed the prisoner, then updated Cahill from St George – it was a reflection of the crime's importance that his reports went straight to the commissioner.

Accused is on remand and in custody...He is a jackaroo on Doondi station of which with other stations his uncle Alan Jeffray of Brisbane is the managing director. Vernon is 25 years of age, native of Scotland about 12 months in this state. He has been in South Africa and he stated a member of the Cape Mounted Police. He left South Africa in 1908. He is of shorten stature and nuggety build, light brown hair and clean shaven. The murdered man John Neil is said to be a native of Clarence River, NSW, about 65 years of age, stout build, 5 ft 8 in, fair complexion, grey hair whiskers and moustache...He was much respected by all classes and trusted by his employers, he has been at Doondi about four years.

Next day, Daley moved on to Doondi, where McGuire and Quinlan were belatedly standing guard. He summed the situation up quickly. He studied the personnel. He studied the terrain. He had his men sketch and diagram the station. He evaluated his exhibits against what might also exist. As he advised Cahill:

I have learned since coming here that the accused is believed to be wearing a whitish colour pyjamas when he committed the deed. I have therefore set out to ascertain the number of suits the accused owned or was known to own and I find from Mrs Burdekin, who used to make up the accused's bedroom, that she only knew of 3 suits: two of whitish colour same material and one pair of silky material with a pink stripe. This is the suit the accused was wearing before the tragedy and Mrs Burdekin put them under his pillow on the morning of the 23rd ultimo when making up his bed. This pair are not among the accused's effects and they cannot be found. I am strongly of the opinion it is the pair he wore when he committed and that the few bloodstains on the pyjamas now sent to Brisbane for examination probably occurred when he was changing from one suit to another. The state of the deceased's bedroom show the walls besmeared with blood half way to the ceiling and the accused's clothing whatever they were should be saturated with blood.

Suspecting that George might have tossed the bloodied pyjamas into the Balonne, Daley instructed McGuire and Quinlan to begin dragging the river with grappling irons from a row boat. It was a bold conjecture: the waterway was up to six metres deep. But after a couple of days, the waters gave up a twine-tied package containing pyjamas that bore, on the left front pocket and waistband, the name 'G. Vernon'. They were stained with mud rather than blood, but the manner of their discarding occasioned suspicion, and Daley ordered McGuire to take them to Brisbane. 'Re Doondi murder,' the sergeant wired Cahill. 'Situation improving.'

Potentially 'the best evidence', Daley realised, was from the Burdekins – eyewitnesses trumped every physical artefact and all circumstantial reasoning. But the cook and housekeeper were, he noted, an odd couple. Ralph Burdekin was thirty-seven. His origins were obscure. He claimed to be from Sydney, to have droved and shorn in Queensland for twenty years on half a dozen stations, and otherwise to rely on a small legacy. But when Daley interviewed him for the first time, Burdekin appeared furtive, secretive, conspiratorial, alternating, as he had with Brown, between hesitancy and bravado. 'I was not satisfied with the interview,' Daley reported to Cahill guardedly. 'I felt that Burdekin was holding back something he saw or knew. He is a man of peculiar disposition and will require careful handling.' Three days later, Daley and Burdekin spoke again, with slightly better results, although Daley's update to Cahill again offered only qualified endorsement: 'I have had a further interview with him today and I am fairly satisfied he will when giving evidence identify the accused as the person he saw set fire to the deceased's bed valance.'

Daley pressed on. In a third interview the next day, he reported, Burdekin remained hesitant: 'The night was bright and the blaze from the fire in the room lit the place up. Burdekin then formed the opinion that the man he saw was the accused but he will not swear it.' Finally, two days later, in a fourth interview, Burdekin came good. 'I had a further interview with Burdekin after posting the [previous] report,' Daley reported. 'I now hold his written statement identifying the accused George Vernon as the man he saw come out the door of the deceased's bedroom.'

Even so, it was hardly the set of cast-iron certainties the police had hoped for, and Isabella was still more equivocal. She was subdued, anxious, sometimes teary. Born in Scotland, raised in Charleville, she had married Burdekin, three years her elder, in Roma in February 1907; around him, she seldom spoke. She even provided Daley with evidence that might be of assistance to the suspect, narrating how, some weeks before, George had come into the kitchen complaining of having been kicked in the chin by a horse. When she applied boracic and lard to the wound, George had said: 'Don't change the pillow case on my bed. There is blood on it and there may be more blood on it yet.' George's defence counsel, Daley acknowledged, might rely on this incident as a potential alternative origin of the blood on the exhibits. The forensic evidence would hardly be unimpeachable in any event. The anti-serum tests of government bacteriologist, C. J. Pound, could only establish to a reasonable accuracy whether blood was human rather than animal, not whose it was.

Such was the harsh reality of outback policing a hundred and more years ago: clumsy constables, unreliable witnesses, primitive forensics, and attenuated lines of communication across vast, vast distances. Savage was never able to get to Doondi. He had been invalided in a fall from a horse some months earlier and was shortly to take early retirement. His replacement, Toowoomba-based Inspector James Geraghty, was a vastly experienced officer, who had risen steadily through the ranks since joining the force as a constable in

FIRST-CLASS INSPECTOR GERAGHTY.

December 1877. But nor was he a well man, suffering recurrences of Dengue Fever from his years in the tropics; he was also recently widowed, his wife having died of pneumonia a few months earlier.

The sorriest misfortune was Daley's. Despatched to St George, he had left behind in Roma wife Mary and nine children, one of whom, a daughter, was sick; on 25 October, in his continued absence, she died. In his police personnel file remains a copy of a letter to commissioner Cahill politely seeking reimbursement for the expense: 'My wife sent me telephone messages of her condition amounting to £1-10-11, which amount Constable Ferguson the clerk paid out of the stamp account. I shall be thankful if the Commissioner would be pleased to authorise the amount.'

With the arrival of George Vernon's legal representative, matters would complicate further.

*

To act for George, Alan Jeffray had retained the large Brisbane firm of J. F. Fitzgerald & Power. As their advance guard, they despatched Ralph Dyball, an experienced criminal solicitor with the firm Dyball & Thompson based in Roma. Dyball, fifty-one, was a strangely apt choice for his client. At George's age, he had been charged with misconduct in the handling of a client's mortgage, and been struck off the solicitor's roll; a few years later, however, he had applied successfully for readmission, and formed a partnership with F. W. B. Thompson. When

R. H. DYBALL.
(Accused's Solicitor).

Dyball arrived at St George Police Station on 10 November and met his client, etiolated and weakened from a six-week confinement in which he had been mandatorily leg-ironed, he must have felt a pang of sympathy. This response would have been strengthened by George's convincing adamance about his innocence.

When the committal hearings finally began in the St George Police Court two days later, Dyball made clear that the Australian Pastoral Company would vigorously defend its Englishman. His argument was that the police had made only cursory enquiries, and explored no alternative hypotheses consistent with his client's innocence: in other words, these outback rubes had arrested George before even questioning him, let alone scanning his room or the crime scene, thereby ruining the chances of a thorough investigation.

Geraghty now found himself under pressure. As proceedings cycled through twenty-one witnesses, the case slowed almost to a stop, not only thanks to Dyball's frequent objections but also the laborious stenography of the elderly justice of the peace, Alfred Cornish, used to settling local misdemeanours not presiding in a high-profile homicide. 'I was never connected with a murder case in which I had such an experience as in this,' Geraghty, whose experience of homicide cases went back twenty years, would complain. 'The local justice taking the depositions was a slow writer and not quick at remembering what the witness had stated and I had to be very watchful to try and get the evidence recorded and in this I was not too successful.' Until a specialist depositions clerk was summoned from Dalby, the resulting depositions were painfully confusing and repetitive; the company probably obtained a better sense of proceedings from the station inspector Thomas Brown, who was present every day taking copious notes.

Geraghty claimed George Vernon's conduct in the wake of the attack of Neil as evidence of a *mens rea* (guilty mind). Witness after witness agreed that the defendant 'did not appear anxious to facilitate the removal of Neil to hospital or sending for the police'. Said Sutherland: 'He never suggested anything for his comfort.' Said Lyons: 'I never heard him do anything for his comfort.'

And Ralph Burdekin, as Cornish recorded in his stilted record, was now standing firmly by his identification. 'It was a moonlight night on 23 September 1910,' Burdekin reiterated, describing the apparition in Neil's room he had seen by the additional flare of the match.

> When the light was struck I saw form of man dressed in white his back towards me...The man had his hands above his head and a light in his hands, his hands were together. I saw the light applied by that man to the valance hanging down from the top of the bed. The light being applied, that part of the bed burst into flames and lighted up room. When room was in that condition I saw the man walk out of this room towards corner of garden. By the light of the moon and the light from fire in room I recognised the man as accused George Vernon.

Yet there remained key vulnerabilities in the crown case. Can one, for example, recognise a man at a distance by his back? The cook's evidence was bound to be sternly challenged when the matter went to trial, and his character too. The other witnesses? They were a rough and ready crew –

unlettered, taciturn and coarse. George's consistent proclamations of innocence were at odds with Drew's report that had him more or less admitting his guilt on the night in question; Neil's recorded denials that he knew who had hit him were at odds with Sutherland's recollection that the old man had blamed George. The testimony of both Drew and Sutherland had also to be assessed in light of their admissions of thirsty drinking on the night in question, plus a hint of collusion. In Sutherland's evidence, he described a conversation with Drew after his returning from the horse paddock with a mount: 'One of these I caught and when I came out of the yard the man Drew, a station hand who was there, called me to one side and said to me, (That the defendant had told him that he had knocked him on the head, meaning Neil).' Had that influenced the testimony Sutherland gave in the court in St George about his interaction with Neil?

Sutherland: I said: 'Who hit you with the bat?' And the deceased said: 'He did.'

Geraghty: Who was 'he'?

Sutherland: When the deceased said 'he did' it,

he pointed with his left hand, and the person pointed at was the accused.

Wanting to believe Sutherland, Geraghty had to come up with an explanation: he offered that Neil, in his denials of George's involvement, later acted out of loyalty to his boss.

> The deceased John Neil was a quiet respectable old man and from what I could learn of him I am satisfied that he was trying to shield Vernon when being interviewed by Constable Cullen and had he recovered from injuries he would not be inclined to prosecute lest it might cause any trouble to Mr Higginson, the manager of Doondi, to whom Neil was very much attached.

In the meantime, Geraghty went on fretting over the exhibits – the 'loose way' they were handled on the three-coach journey to Brisbane, meaning they would be 'of little service in the interests of the case'. He complained to Cahill:

> The majority of the exhibits other than the cricket bat – the most important – and a suit of pyjamas found in the river were carelessly handled by police at St George. Mr Dyball, accused's solicitor, who had visited Doondi soon after the

tragedy had knowledge of this; however you will please notice by the remaining depositions, copy of which will be forwarded you in a few days, that I did all I could to cure such neglect.

Still, when Cornish at length committed George for trial in the first sessions of the Queensland Supreme Court the following year, Geraghty wired confidently: 'Prosecution consider case clear.' Cahill echoed him: 'This case was bungled in a deplorable manner by the St George police but I am confident that everything possible has been done by Inspector Geraghty to remedy the serious errors that have been made.'

George Vernon turned twenty-five, then spent Christmas, in gaol. He had known some ignominy in his short life, but this was perhaps the nadir: he had landed in a nation of convicts and become one. Australia's successors to Port Arthur and Norfolk Island had similarly evocative epithets: Pentridge, Long Bay, Yatala. But none, perhaps, was quite so resonant as HM Prison Brisbane, traditionally known by the location set aside for it in 1880: Boggo Road.

Boggo Road was a hard place, often stiflingly hot, with a characteristic odor of canteen hominy and laundry sulphur. All the requisite customs of Edwardian penology were observed. Labour was menial – either picking oakum, making mats or plaiting straw (for hats). Deprivations were petty – the prohibition on knives and forks, an inmate complained, forced prisoners to 'eat like an aboriginal or a Fijian cannibal.'

It was only eight years since a separate women's prison had been built, and men in the yard circulated fairly freely: prisoners awaiting trial, like George, got around with first offenders and long-time men alike. But once the cell door closed, the walls closed in. During George's time there, *Truth* printed a multi-part insider's account, replete with gruesome detail.

> The furniture of each cell consists of a quart pot (filled with water), a small wooden stool, a spoon, and for sleeping purposes a hammock with about five blankets. Some of these blankets are worn, to the consistency of tissue paper. As one wag remarked, 'You could drag them from here to Bathurst without picking up a burr.' When the door is closed, the bolts shot, and the keys turned in the lock, you fondly imagine you will be left alone for the night to 'whip the cat' or sleep, as the fancy takes you; BUT NOT SO. "Hands up" is roared out in a stentorian voice, with a brogue that you could cut with a spade, and Chief Warder Murphy goes round to every call — each prisoner having to show his hand at the grating over the door — to show that none of the birds are missing, and every cage has its occupant.

Overleaf: Vernon (second from top) in the Boggo Road register

Most men were on relatively short sentences: in Boggo slang, one month was 'a moon', three months 'a drag', six months 'a zack', twelve months 'a stretch', five years 'a fin'. So a capital crime singled George out, and he walked in the shadow of a disturbingly busy scaffold. In its first four decades, Boggo Road had hosted roughly a hanging a year; there had been seventeen in the first decade of the twentieth century. Public opinion about the death penalty in Queensland had actually been shifting. There had been a spasm of discomfiture at the 1909 execution of twenty-year-old Arthur Ross, who had more or less accidentally shot a clerk in a bank robbery as they grappled for a revolver. When Queensland's executive council ignored a jury's recommendation of mercy, baby-faced Ross had gone to the gallows with moving contrition, to the point of writing a letter of condolence to the clerk's parents: 'I am sorry I killed such a brave young man and in forfeiting my life I am only getting what I deserve.' Even Alexander Bradshaw, who had cold-bloodedly shot up his mistress's family at Carron River, elicited sympathy from *Truth* for the ghastly theatre of his execution in June 1910.

Up the fateful steps to the gallows they [Bradshaw, the chaplain and warders] went, and presently the prisoner, pallid and trembling, was placed on the fatal trap-door. He was a slightly-built man, with reddish-yellow hair and whiskers, 5ft. 8¾in. in height, and aged only 28 years. His peculiarly-shaped head, was eloquent of weak, of almost non-existent mentality. While his bonds were being adjusted, he displayed some little perturbation, and once a warder had to speak to him about moving, as his gestures suggested that he was making up his mind for a bolt. At last, when the rope had been placed loosely over his neck, and all was ready, he was asked if he wished to say anything. For a short space he was silent; then, in a voice unnaturally calm, he recited a brief prayer. The white cap was drawn over the face, a handkerchief dropped silently, the hangman touched the lever, and then ensued a gruesome and ghastly sight. As the body reached the end of the drop blood fell in a stream, covering the floor for yards around, and completely saturating the clothes of the corpse. Hastily, officials rushed with sawdust, two boxes of which were emptied over the spot. The head of the unfortunate man was found, on examination, to be almost torn from the body.

George could console himself that strenuous efforts were being made in his defence: the Australian Pastoral Company's legal expenses would swell to four figures. Alan Jeffray provided unstinting support. Bill Young, temporarily based on Noondoo, paid for Dyball to spend weeks on Doondi, to the growing discomfiture of occupants, Arthur Higginson and Ralph Burdekin in particular. Soon after Dyball left around Christmas, in fact, there was an unspecified incident which resulted in the station manager dismissing his cook. Much to Isabella's distress, she and her husband had to head north looking for work.

Was this to do with the case? It is unclear. What is apparent is that Fitzgerald & Power recognised Burdekin as the crown's most dangerous witness, and were intent on gleaning as much as possible about him: St George's *Balonne Beacon* would write suggestively of 'the expenditure of a liberal supply of money from London' in pursuit of evidence favourable to the defence. Burdekin claimed to have worked on several stations over two decades in Queensland, from Aramac, near Longreach, to Ardglen, near Cunnamulla. Fitzgerald &

Power committed to comprehensively retracing his steps, and also to nosing round Doondi – to Higginson's growing irritation. In a letter dated 7 January 1911, now among the company's mortal documentary remains in the State Library of Queensland, Young effectively scolded his station manager for a lack of cooperation.

Dear Arthur,

Vernon's solicitors have just advised me that they propose sending a man from Brisbane to Doondi in connection with his trial and have asked me if the company had any objection. I have explained that far from my having any objection I will be only too glad to give their man every assistance to collect any information they may require. Rightly or wrongly they convey to me their impression that you will resent their man's obtaining at Doondi any information they require. I cannot think that it is so and am sorry your behaviour in the matter should have given them this impression but one point I am quite clear upon is this, namely, when I approve of anyone going to Doondi, he must be treated by you as a guest of mine should be treated. If your feelings are so wrong on this matter, as they apparently are, that you cannot be amicable to this man who is being up with the object, I presume, of collecting what evidence he can in refutation of the evidence against Vernon then I would suggest your absenting yourself from Doondi during his visit but I trust you will not feel this necessary.

The police were busy with their case also, the better to know their quarry.

The telegraph enabled Geraghty to solicit information about George Vernon from the British African Police in Rhodesia, the Mounted Rifles in Canada and colleagues at Scotland Yard. The Metropolitan Police went to the trouble, on Geraghty's request, of seeking out old cricket colleagues of George's father. Lord Hawke, about to play his last season for Yorkshire, and Alexander Webbe, now secretary at Middlesex, duly swore by their friend's boy.

Scotland Yard confirm your records George Vernon son of well known cricketer both parents dead Lord Hawke promised father look after lad always interested in welfare and informs police has known Vernon from childhood last saw him eighteen months ago

MEMORANDUM

Ask Chief Secretary to
have cable sent to Chief of Police
Scotland Yard to ascertain
if anything known to police
of previous history & character
of the accused Vernon. give
description.

To Scotland Yard

Chief Police

OTTAWA.

George Vernon committed trial here wilful murder aged twenty-five
native Scotland educated five feet four light hair clean shaven
strong muggety build was rafting mining Canada, served Canadian
Mounted Rifles January February nought-nine. please cable
anything known history character.

Cahill Commissioner Police.

Commr. of Police, Brisbane, Q.
24/1/11.

To Ottawa

Original to
Crow Soler.
1.2.11.

£6

TELEGRAPH STATION
1 FE 11
G.P.O.

No. 4.
En bon   29 Salisbury Rhodesia 31st   7 WR

Commissioner Police Brisbane Qld

Vernon served in police period Mentioned your
telegram secured discharge by purchase was
Convicted five times drunkenness during
this period otherwise nothing known against
him

455 am 1ff   Police

From Salisbury

From

To

From

To

ANSWER.

OFFICE OF THE CHIEF OF POLICE, WINNIPEG. JAN 1911

Winnipeg Jan 26 1911 _____ 19

I hereby certify that George Vernon was discharged by purchase (being under three months) from Strathcona's Horse (R C) on the 22nd day of February 1909. His character was good.

N B Kettle,
Colonel.
Commanding Strathcona's Horse
(R C)

The corps was now styled Ro R. C. M Rifles

N B Kettle

MB. Form B ...
200 M—...
H.Q. 1772-29 BB.

From Winnipeg

before started for Queensland desires you to know has always regarded Vernon as highly respectable and intelligent nothing known detrimentally his conduct while in England or abroad Webbe Godfather states Cecil Rhodes was also interested him and describes him as of good chivalrous disposition had news that he was on good terms with everybody at Station reports received by Police from other influential persons all favourable.

Elsewhere, police were handicapped that some witnesses had now dispersed in the course of their duties: Cullen had to be sent all the way to Angledool in New South Wales to locate Ah Chow, only to find that the Chinese supplier could not lay his hands on the invoice proving the theft of the whisky. Then, in Maranoa, it rained, hard. By mid-January, the Condamine had burst its banks. Low-lying areas flooded; there were heavy stock losses; a boy at Warwick and young stockman at Chinchilla drowned; mails were delayed and bridges submerged. Doondi was cut off, both from St George, and from the nearest railway station, at Yeulba 220km north. First the balance of the exhibits including most of the contents of Neil's room, then the majority of the witnesses, were marooned; nor could a locum filling in for Dr Elliott get to St George. Finally, as rains abated after nearly a month, Higginson, Drew and Bowman embarked for Surat, where council workers were rowing travellers across the swollen Condamine, while the horses swam across to connect with another coach.

Yeulba existed only because of the Western Line. The hamlet by the platform was so small that, a few years later, when a railway carpenter misspelled the location as 'Yuleba', it was deemed easier to change the place name. Slowly but slowly the parties converged on their legal rendezvous. The Burdekins came from Toowoomba. Others arrived via Mitchell and via Talwood. The prosecution remained confident. 'On the whole,' Geraghty advised Cahill, 'I consider that the evidence disclosed by the depositions establishes a strong case of Wilful Murder against the accused.'

5

'THE UTTER UNRELIABITY OF THE WITNESS'

In 1911, Brisbane had officially been a city only nine years, and its population of 130,000 supported only sixty barristers. One among them was in constant demand. People joked that Arthur Feez KC had a highly suitable name for a barrister, except that the surname was pronounced 'Fates', which was perhaps even more suitable. His career may itself have been fated. He was the grandson of the first resident judge of the Moreton Bay District, whose daughter had married into a well-to-do mercantile family with Bavarian ancestry. Educated

ARTHUR FEEZ, K.C.,
BARRISTER-AT-LAW.
Thou wouldst be great;
Art not without ambition.
—Shakespeare,
"Macbeth," Act I, Scene 6.

A barrister, and eke K.C.,
A skilled and powerful pleader,
A student deep of law is he,
And of the Bar a leader.
Among the Commonwealth's elite
No man, in Austral States,
Is surer soon to take his seat
On Judge's Bench than Feez.

at King's School and Sydney University, Feez had joined the Queensland Bar aged twenty-one, and within two decades become its dominant figure. Crime was not his speciality; he was most at home in the realms of estates, tax, finance and fraud. But in pleading he was renowned for his courtesy and urbanity, and in cross-examination he had been likened to a terrier after a rat.

Tall and rather grand, Feez was also a clubbable Queensland personality. An enthusiastic rugby footballer, golfer and cricketer, he had been an early chairman of the colony's first cricket association. He was a member of the Brisbane Racing Club, a committeeman at the Brisbane Hunt Club, a selector at the Brisbane Polo Club. He had served as a Rhodes Scholarship selection panellist, as a councillor of the Tuberculosis Prevention Society, and as chancellor of the Synod of the Anglican diocese of Brisbane. Feez combined his status as a social lion with being a patron of the arts – he was a friend of the dancer Anna Pavlova, an intimate of the musical Carandini family, and had acted as Charles Armstrong's best man at his wedding to Nellie Melba. His wife Fanny, the daughter of Brisbane's leading solicitor, was known for her hospitality: their Indooroopilly family home, Coorabel, was ever a venue for balls, luncheons, fetes and garden parties. Feez tackled even commuting with a certain style. He was chauffeured daily to Lutwyche Chambers in Adelaide Street in a five-seat Ford tourer – a suitable marque for the president of the Queensland Automotive Club.

Feez kept a diary – not a journal of intimate thoughts, but a chatty recitation of his professional engagements, social doings and their intersection. His becoming the inaugural president of the Bar Association of Queensland, for example, occasioned the following sample entry.

12 June 1903

Court at 10 in *Kingston v Robt Reid & Co.* when the second action was finally disposed of, leave being given to compound it. Meeting of Bar Committee at 11 and at 12 I had a conference with Chambers and Smith Manager of Burns Philp & Co. Game of snooker after lunch and I played better. Bar meeting in the AG's chambers when we formed a Bar Association and passed certain resolutions. It was a fair

> meeting. Our wedding anniversary Fan gave
> me a matchbox and I her an opera clock. Wiley
> to dinner and stayed yarning till past 10.30.
> Very pleasant and happy day.

How Feez came to represent George Vernon is unknown, but it is hardly difficult to guess. Feez and Jeffray were both members of the Queensland Club; their wives featured regularly on the 'Gossip from Women's Clubland' page of *Queensland Figaro*; Feez was a close friend of Jeffray's brother-in-law Allan Macnaughton. Since the Gatton murders, too, Queensland had developed a certain affinity for murder trials with faraway backdrops. The public were titillated, inconclusively, when an Indigenous station hand, Billy Wilson, was accused of slashing the throat of governess Nellie Duffy on Carpentaria Downs station in September 1908: Wilson made no fewer than three different 'confessions', for none of which, two juries agreed, there was the remotest proof. No case since had occasioned such public fascination as the murder of John Neil. Feez received his 'permission to act' in *R v Vernon* on 28 January and first surveyed the brief on 14 February, mentioning it in his Letts'

Australasian Scribbling Diary as a task to occupy him at home while he nursed an ankle tender from gout. Two days later, 'ankle much better', he accompanied Dyball to Boggo Road for a two-hour meeting with his client.

By now, of course, George had spent ten weeks in gaol, which had been gruelling but had the serendipitous effect of depriving him of alcohol. Still and sober in his prison greys, he stuck straightforwardly to a story of going to bed after a friendly encounter with Neil, and not awaking until the stir after midnight. And what about this was so difficult to believe? Feez was 'very much impressed.' It may have been then, over lunch at Lennon's Hotel on George Street, that Dyball shared with Feez the fruits of Fitzgerald & Power's investigations of the crown's star witness, Ralph Burdekin.

After lunch, Feez re-entered court for the resumption of hearings involving the damages from the stranding of a steamer, *Wairarapa* – coincidentally before the same judge designated to hear *R v Vernon*. Acting Chief Justice Patrick Real had been senior puisne judge of the Supreme Court for eight years, the culmination of a remarkable self-made life. His tenant farmer father had died on the family's journey from Limerick in 1851, when Real was four; young Patrick was first a carpenter's apprentice then a railway worker, and only able to turn to the law after training in Latin and Greek from a kindly clergyman. Real became a presence at the Bar thanks to Sir Samuel Griffith's preference for him as a junior; his gruff voice and grey beard had made him a formidable figure on the bench. His attitude in the *Wairarapa* matter reminded Feez how much he disliked Real; the judge was arrogant, garrulous and obtuse. Still later, Feez had his first conference with his own junior, John Woolcock, and the following afternoon another 'long consultation' ahead of what loomed as a fierce encounter – albeit one that would not begin on time. Marooned by the muddy roads and swollen rivers of the flooded Darlings Downs, many witnesses had still to arrive.

Feez, frankly, was concerned. The press would be intense; the judge would be a nuisance; juries were unpredictable; the client, effectively the Australian Pastoral Company, was prestigious.

On the evening of Wednesday 22 February 1911, the night before proceedings finally commenced, he dined with Dyball at the Brisbane Club and had another lengthy consultation with Woolcock. Afterwards he confided in his diary that the 'Murder Case' was 'worrying me awfully', and referred to Sutherland, Drew and Burdekin as 'the deadly witnesses.' The fight of George Vernon's life would be the fight of Arther Feez's career.

*

'It was a moonlight night,' began Tiny Sutherland, the first witness sworn in.

Crowds had begun assembling early that morning at the iron gates on George Street that guarded the main entrance of Queensland's Supreme Court; as proceedings opened, there was a sizeable audience in the public gallery, craning their necks for a view as George Vernon was brought up from the cells. Commissioner William Cahill and Inspector James Geraghty eyeballed the defendant; Alan Jeffray and Allan Macnaughton were there for their young friend. Nobody had forgotten his patrimony. This was, noted the *Gympie Times*, a case mingling the glamour of sport with the trappings of wealth.

> Accused is a well educated young Englishman who was jackerooing on the station. His father is the well-known English cricketer, George Vernon, one of the most brilliant batsmen of his day, who visited Australia and Queensland with Ivo Bligh's team in 1883. Vernon here met the lady who was destined to become his future wife in Melbourne during the tour of the team and became engaged to her...It is a coincidence that, according to the sworn evidence, the murdered man on two or three occasions stated in explanation of the murderous assault which culminated in his death that he had been hit on the head with a cricket bat. An uncle of accused on his mother's side is the manager of the Brisbane branch of a large Australian trading firm. It is said that considerable interest is being evinced in the trial in high places.

Truth's vigilant correspondent offered a near-phrenological interpretation of the twenty-five-year-old's appearance: 'Vernon is a young man, with the face of a boy; large, blue eyes slightly prominent; fair and good-looking, with a shapely, clean-cut head and profile; short in stature, but well built with broad shoulders. He followed the proceedings with intense interest, and when he first came into the dock took a calm survey of the Court and the persons assembled there. He wore a heavy, well-cut, grey suit, turned down collar, and was well groomed.' His response to the reading of the indictment was to deliver a plea of 'Not Guilty' in a 'clear, calm, firm voice.' He gave close attention to the opening addresses of Crown Prosecutor Jonathan Kingsbury, and to Sutherland's methodical recapitulation of the events of 23 September.

Feez had a plan, to persuade the shearer to concede that drink might have muddied his recollection. He was unable to budge Sutherland from his recollection of Neil had fingered George. 'Neil did know who did it,' Sutherland said, pointing at George. 'He told me he did it.' But perhaps, he conceded, he had slightly misheard George's remarks about not going for the police; perhaps it had been a remark about the importance of getting medical attention. The judge, as Feez anticipated, was querulous. 'Commenced *R v*

Vernon which is worrying the life out of me,' Feez reported in his diary. 'Old Real was very talkative while I was XXg Sutherland but I kept good temper. Jeffray drove me to the club for lunch.' Afterwards, Sutherland yielded to the judge's inquiries about the influence of alcohol.

> Real: Why did you have a drink that night?
>
> Sutherland: Wouldn't you have a nip if you saw a man dying in front of you?
>
> Feez: It would be likely to upset Vernon then.
>
> Sutherland: It did upset him very much. There was blood all over the room. The walls were splashed with it.

It was then Woolcock's turn to run foul of the judge. McCoy supported Sutherland's story of Neil's accusation against George ('He did it with a bat'), but also conceded possibly misunderstanding George's aversion to calling the law ('Vernon said: "I don't know what the police have to do with it. I think it is a case for the doctor" ') and taking a drink or two ('It was a horrible sight, and a glass of grog was a very welcome thing under the circumstances'). But trying to accentuate a slight inconsistency in McCoy's deposition about who was present at the time the night horse was fetched, Feez's junior incurred Real's wrath.

BARRISTER WOOLCOCK

Real: It did not seem to me to be inconsistent.

Woolcock: It seemed to me to be so.

Real: Perhaps I have had more experience than you.

Woolcock: I am not so familiar with these incidents as this man.

Real: Why not? You have read all those papers. You ought to know more about them than he does.

Woolcock: I am sorry I made a slip.

Real: We are all fallible. You may not have thought you were but now you know.

The defence was barely hanging on. *Truth* thought that the defendant was visibly aging: 'On this day, Vernon, who is only 24 years of age [sic], looked careworn and spent, most of the time standing in a corner of the dock, following every word that was spoken and keenly keeping his eyes fixed on the witness.' When Charlie Drew commenced his evidence in chief, Feez himself began to feel unwell. It was the first hint of a bout of Dengue Fever, having one of its periodic flare-ups in Brisbane, after an outright epidemic six years earlier. By Sunday, when Feez awoke in a febrile sweat at 3.30am and recorded a temperature of 103 degrees, he was in the grip of the disease. It was an inopportune moment to be diarising: 'Could do nothing.'

'Very ill today,' Feez began his diary entry for Monday 27 February, but nobody would have been any the wiser, as he set out to destroy Drew. The bush worker was a 'deadly witness' because he claimed that George had more or less confessed to him when they went to purloin the first of those several whisky bottles. But for Feez, he was a relatively easy mark. Sinewy, leathery, moustachioed, with a 'Faith, hope and charity' tattoo on one bicep, he looked out of place in a witness stand. First, Feez [first] had him admit at least 'five drinks' on the fateful night, with a hint of the possibility of more.

Feez: Didn't you nearly fall off your horse?

Drew: It is correct to say I was quite sober, only excited.

Feez: How many bottles were drunk that night?

Drew: Three bottles as far as I know.

Feez: As a matter of fact there were more than three bottles drunk that night.

Next, he cajoled Drew into conceding the impact on his recollection of being 'a bit on the groggy side'.

Feez: I suppose that you were glad to get as much as you could that night.

Drew: Well, I would not refuse it.

Feez: Do you really remember what took place that night?

Drew: No, not all the time.

Then, Feez sprang a trap, confusing Drew into misremembering exactly when George had 'confessed' to him

Feez: Are you not aware that you put that episode of the confession before Vernon and Bowman went for the horse? Now you put it after.

Drew: I don't remember...It may have been a long time before. I have the time wrong. I have not been told that I have made a mess of my evidence. It is the other way round. I have been complimented on it.

Most importantly, with regard to George's 'confession', Feez challenged Drew about his under reaction.

Feez: Do you mean to tell me seriously that you made no remark when the prisoner said this?

Drew: I was too surprised to say anything.

Feez: You weren't too surprised to help him to get the bottle of whisky?

Drew: No.

Feez: You weren't too surprised to go round a second time to steal more Chinaman's whisky, and to help Vernon drink it.

Drew: No.

'I don't think Drew carried much weight after I finished with him,' Feez diarised with satisfaction. He had neutralised Sutherland and destroyed Drew; now for Burdekin.

*

Sutherland had been significant in the Crown case and Drew important but Burdekin, that man of 'peculiar disposition', was essential. Taking the stand in the hushed court, he cut an unprepossessing figure: *Truth* called him 'a smallish, insignificant, middle-aged man, who looked like a ship's steward'. Kingsbury gave him the 'careful handling' that Daley had recommended, leading him gently through his dramatic testimony, including its identification of George Vernon as the man who had lit the valance. The accused followed as intently as anyone, looking 'as if the terrible ordeal, which he is now undergoing, was beginning to tell on him...His eyes appeared sleepless, and his young, rounded face had a drawn look.' Feez was sicker still. As he rose to cross-examine, enrobed and bewigged in the stifling court, his face was slick with the perspiration of his fever. But soon it would be Burdekin sweating.

> Feez: You have a marvellous memory, have you not?
>
> Burdekin: I don't know that I have.
>
> Feez: Have you learned your evidence by heart?
>
> Burdekin: (indignantly) No I have not!

Feez challenged him immediately with a statement from the station inspector Thomas Brown, who visiting Doondi a few days after the murder had caught Burdekin's initial hesitancy about the identification. Burdekin started back-pedalling, denying the conversation had taken place, then saying that he 'could not remember it', then insisting that he had not told Brown 'that I saw a man coming out of Neil's room in what looked like white clothes but I could not distinguish the man'. The Crown seems to have been caught completely unawares. Kingsbury said nothing. Only Real tried to intervene. 'I do not see that all this is material,' the judge blustered.

'Your honour's mind must be very dense, I am sorry to say it,' retorted Feez, not even slightly sorry.

Feez had more. George's lawyers had obtained a statement from a boundary rider, Tom Moody, recalling a conversation with Burdekin soon after the murder in which the cook had said 'he saw a match struck and a man in white, but he could not make out who it was.' Burdekin, non-plussed, continued to insist that he was a truthful witness, but his confidence had clearly taken a knock.

Feez then launched into a fierce attack on Burdekin's pedigree. Burdekin had given the registrar a birthplace of Sydney, a father's name of

Harold Sydney Burdekin and/or Sydney Burdekin, and a mother's maiden name of Eveline Thorn. He had claimed childhood addresses in Lower Macquarie Street and Little Castlereagh Street.

> Feez: I suppose it would astonish you to hear that no person of the name of Harold Sydney Burdekin can be traced to Sydney?
>
> Burdekin: No...Your Honour, is it necessary to drag the names of my parents into this?
>
> Feez: When I say anything derogatory about your parents you can stop me.
>
> Real: Go on, Mr Feez, it is all right.
>
> Feez: What occupation did your father follow?
>
> Burdekin: He followed no occupation.
>
> Feez: What do you mean?
>
> Burdekin: I never saw him do any work.

Laughter rippled round the court. Burdekin shrank further.

> Feez: Did you live in style?

Burdekin: In fair circumstances.

Feez: Did you keep a horse and trap?

Burdekin: No.

Feez: How many servants did you keep?

Burdekin: None.

Feez: Would you be surprised to know that there is no record of Ralph Burdekin being being born in Sydney between January 1 1864 and December 31 1890?

Burdekin: I don't know anything about that.

It was a remarkable jag in a cross-examination, and it continued, as Feez claimed that there were no such places in Sydney as 'Lower Macquarie Street' and 'Little Castlereagh Street'. Feez then went through Burdekin's account of his movement in Queensland, quibbling over every detail. When Burdekin said he had boarded for a time in Queen Street between George and Albert Streets, Feez scoffed: 'I have lived in Brisbane thirty years and I never remember a boarding house in that part

of Queen Street.' Equally astonishing is that
Kingsbury did nothing to intervene, and that
Real complained only about the 'waste of time'
involved rather than the dubious relevance of the
interrogation.

> Feez: I am trying to show the utter unreliability
> of the witness.
>
> Real: You can go on as long as you like. If it
> was anything other than a murder case I would
> have stopped it long ago. I would not have sat
> here for four hours finding out what his father's
> and mother's names were.
>
> Feez: It is very kind of your Honour to say so.
> I intend to do what I consider to be proper in
> the case. If I occupied three hours' time more I
> would not consider it wasted.

Establishing Burdekin's unreliability, in
fact, was only part of Feez's purpose; nobody in
court would have missed the additional purport
of the counsel's questions, which was the doubt
they cast on the witness's legitimacy. It was
hardly unknown for a birth to go unregistered

in Australia, but what it usually denoted was that parents were unmarried. There is a further additional possibility, in Burdekin's reluctance to 'drag the names of my parents in'. His marriage certificate gives his father's name, unambiguously, as Sydney Burdekin. At least some in the jury would have recognised this name as that of the wealthy squatter and landlord who had served as Lord Mayor of Sydney twenty years earlier. Ralph Burdekin assented that his father was deceased, that he had read of his death in the *Town and Country Journal*. In December 1899, the *Journal* had indeed reported the death of Sydney Burdekin, 'one of the best known figures' in civic life: 'The deceased, who succumbed to dropsy, leaves a widow, two sons, and three daughters to mourn their loss.' The probable inference of Feez's questions about the 'style' of Burdekin's upbringing was that these five surviving children were not Sydney Burdekin's only offspring – that Ralph Burdekin was a son of the erstwhile mayor's mistress. Illegitimacy had been the original sin of many a remittance man; how ironic if Burdekin was himself an untidy genetic cast off.

The Crown reeled. Kingsbury's clerk, Hubert Harrington, despatched a 'most urgent' letter to Cahill, asking him to wire Sydney counterparts with a series of bulletpoints: 'When did a well-known man in Sydney named Sydney Burdekin die?' 'Is there any entry of birth of a man named Ralph Burdekin in Sydney 10th May 1874 or thereabouts'; 'Did a woman named Eveline Thorn register the birth of a child about the last mentioned date? If so who was alleged to be the father of that child?' Apart from advising Sydney Burdekin's death eleven years earlier, the replies would confirm Feez's findings, and they would be too late to make a difference anyway. Because while Burdekin was perspiring, Feez cast back to the night of 23 September, and arrowed in on the witness's credit from another angle – why had Burdekin sought the assistance of Bowman and Drew before going to Neil's aid?

> Feez: What sort of a man do you call yourself when you leave that man [Neil] in a burning room, while you get help?

> Burdekin: You would do the same if you knew there was a man inside.

Feez: But you said you saw him go outside?

Burdekin: What was to stop him coming back?

Feez: You mean to say that you were such a coward that you would not rush to that burning room to try and save that man?

Burdekin: I would not rush without help.

Then, yet another angle. Feez returned to the history of Burdekin's movements in Queensland, and homed in on the cook's claim to have worked for a time at Aramac, a station leased by Goldsborough Mort, 80km south-east of Muttaburra.

Feez: You told us you worked at Aramac, and that you were engaged by Mr James Tolson. Would you recognise him if you saw him?

Burdekin: Yes.

Feez: I may tell you that he is in court. Have a look round and tell me if you see him.

The courtroom sat in stunned silence. As Burdekin scanned the faces, onlookers tracked his gaze. 'I do not see him in court,' Burdekin said at last.

A figure stepped toward: the Australian Pastoral Company had brought James Tolson 1000km from Aramac just for this purpose. 'You have been looking at him all the time,' said Feez with satisfaction. 'I may as well tell you that Mr Tolson does not recognise you.'

Feez concluded the day by revealing that Burdekin had been dismissed from his position at Doondi. Brisbane's *Daily Mail* caught his faltering admissions: 'Witness was discharged from Doondi on December 31, for what reason he did not know. Mr Higginson dismissed him. Witness did not have a row with him, but Higginson offered to fight him. When Higginson gave him a week's notice he told him he did not know how to cook. He did not know why he was dismissed; it might have been over the present case. He did not know that he had the reputation of being a most positively insolent man to his employers. He had not been very fortunate in his situations. He was not a very jealous man.' Oh yes? demanded his interrogator.

> Feez: Is it not true that when you used to go out on the run for an hour you used to lock up your wife?

Burdekin: No it is not. Bring the person here who says it!

Feez: You did not like anyone to speak to your wife, did you?

Burdekin: No, that is not true.

Feez: Weren't you dismissed from Ardglen because you were ordered out on the run, and you came back without permission to see what your wife was up to?

Burdekin: It is not true!

Real: I think it very extraordinary.

Feez: I am going to do what I have a perfect right to do.

And he had. As Burdekin stepped down from the stand that afternoon, the crown's star witness looked broken, defeated.

The curious reality was that Burdekin's evidence of the fateful night at Doondi had been but little challenged; Feez had hardly mentioned it. It remained open to a jury to believe every word

Burdekin said. Prosecution and defence had both made efforts to recreate the scene on the night of 23 September, to check the possibility of Burdekin having seen what he claimed to have seen. The results had been inconclusive. The prosecution urged that the spreading foliage of a fast-growing cedar in the yard had been a recent development; the defence challenged that the policeman playing the part of the killer in the re-enactment was too tall; everyone knew it had been a 'moonlight night'. But in the end it was the word of a man rather than the light of a moon that had electrified the court. Feez finished the day exhausted: 'Dengue very bad. But had to keep going as I had Burdekin xx.' It had been worth the effort.

6

'THAT CLASS OF BOY'

The tide had turned. Feez returned to court on Wednesday 1 March, but left the questioning of Isabella Burdekin to his junior Woolcock. The prosecution now encountered more resistance from the judge than the defence. Real had allowed senior counsel considerable latitude; he would not extend the junior same. 'This is humbug!' he erupted at one point, as Woolcock challenged Isabella over how else and in what order blood might have made its way onto George's belongings – the injury from the horse, the non-changing of the pillow slip etc. 'I feel it is my duty to stop humbug. I don't care what case it is. When I think it is my duty I will do it. I have been long-suffering and patient.' Woolcock was nettled: 'Well, your honour, I want to cross-examine this witness.' Real was almost beside himself: 'You cannot keep going over and over again!' He promptly adjourned, but was still brooding the next morning.

His Honour, referring to the cross-examination of the witness, said he recognised there was a great strain on counsel in the case, but he could not permit waste of time in asking useless questions, after they had been completely answered, and when the repeating of them could not result in any further light being thrown on the matter.

Woolcock: One must recognise the extreme importance of the case.

His Honour said a quarter of an hour was wasted yesterday afternoon in questioning the witness about the pillowslip. Whether she took the pillowslip off the accused's bed on the Sunday preceding the occurrence or the Sunday following it, or not at all, was of no possible consequence.

Real was only half-right. The defence might not be undermining the Crown case directly, but it was undermining the Crown witnesses. Feez had had to 'cave in' and stay in bed that Thursday, but Woolcock persisted in his stead. Isabella started losing confidence in her recollection, and when Kingsbury returned to re-examine was clearly a pawn in a larger game.

Kingsbury: Have you any idea of the time that elapsed from when you saw Vernon go to feed his dog and when he came back? Can you give a shot at it within fifteen minutes?

Woolcock (objecting): You don't expect the jury to take any notice of 'shots'?

Real: It is all guesswork. I don't know what the jury may think – I don't carry other men's minds in my pocket – but I place no value on times. Sometimes when I have been sitting in this court I think I have been here about five hours but when I look at the clock I find that it has only been about an hour.

In the afternoon, while Woolcock cross-examined Edgar Bowman, Dyball and Jeffray visited Feez, propped up in bed at Coorabel: there would have been general contentment at the way the case was proceeding. Richardson, Berry and Lyons then passed through the stand with little impact. Even the judge seemed subdued as the week wore on, reserving his ire for the Chinese witnesses Ah Chow and Wong Wing.

Ah Chow, who was sworn on a [lit] match, stated that he was a contractor employed at Doondi station, and was working on a contract. He intimated that he wanted an interpreter.

Real: Well, you won't get one. You know all about it.

Ah Chow: I know welly little English.

His Honour said there was an interpreter present and he would be employed if progress could not be made.

AH CHOW.

The duration of the case was starting to take its toll on the jury too. Real had increased their allowances from 8s to a pound a day; on Friday 3 March, he declined their request for a further increase.

Real: Yes, and I am sorry. And I do not know when the case is likely to finish, either.

Foreman: That is the problem.

Real: Anyhow, I will sit tomorrow. If you can find any precedent, I will consider it.

Foreman: We have no means of ascertaining that.

On this additional Saturday morning, the prosecution called Constable Cullen, who recalled his conversations with Neil on what would prove the old man's death bed.

At the hospital witness had conversations with Neil, who said, 'Last night when I went to bed a man came in and struck me with a bat.' I first asked him who the man was, but he said he did not know. Witness asked him if there was any one on the station he thought would do it, and Neil replied in the negative. In further reply to witness, Neil said he had not had a row on the station that day...Witness asked, 'Did you have a row with Vernon while you were drinking with him?' and he replied, 'no'. Witness said, 'Do you think Vernon would do this?' and he replied, 'I don't know what he would do it for.'

It was hardly helpful to the Crown, and Kingsbury by now had subsided into inertia. He had done nothing to protect his witnesses during the enfilade of cross-examination from Feez and Woolcock; in particular he had made no effort, including via Isabella, to repair the damage done to his star witness. The Crown case instead closed mutedly with unenlightening medical evidence from Elliott and unemphatic forensic evidence from Pound, easily rolled back by Feez.

Pound: On the towel there were one or two traces of blood, but I could not say whether they were human or not. I could find no bloodstains on the pyjamas, the handkerchief was blood stained; the blanket was blood-stained and portions of it were burned.

Inventory of articles taken by Constable Cullen from accused's Bedroom showing Blood stains

No	Description
A	A Cricket Bat with Blood stains found by Constable Cullen in accused's Bedroom in a Cricket Bag and claimed by accused as his property
B	A Towel with Blood stains taken by Cullen from accused's Bedroom
C	A Suit of Pyjamas showing Blood stains claimed by accused as his property and stated he was wearing them on night of 31st ultimo.
D	A Pocket Handkerchief found in accused's Coat Breast when search at Lockup St George showing Blood stains
E	Mosquito Net showing Blood stains taken from accused's Bedroom in his Bedroom
F	Piece of Flooring Board taken from floor of Bedroom occupied by accused showing stains
G	Piece of Calico with two Pictures attached showing Blood stains taken from Wall of Room occupied by Deceased.
H	Dark Grey Blanket showing Blood and paint holes taken from Room of the Deceased
I	Matchbox containing what looks like grey hairs and screw found by Acting Sergeant Quinlan outside the Bedroom Window of accused

JR Daley
Sen Sergt 108
4/10/10

167

Feez: Where were the bloodstains on the bat?

Pound: Near the shoulder, on the flat side of the bat, there were some bloodstains, but very infinitesimal, while there were also some on the handle. On the round side of the bat there were three bloodstains, but I had extreme difficulty tracing them as they were small. Immediately below the makers name there was a slight splash...If the bat was lying flat, one of the spots under the right shoulder could be accounted for by blood falling from a bleeding nose or cut chin.

While Kingsbury seemed to be retreating, Feez was busy advancing. He opened the defence's case on Tuesday 7 March with a stirring address.

Whoever was responsible for this murder was guilty of a cruel, monstrous crime. There was no half-way house in this case. The prisoner has either committed wilful murder, or is not guilty. The jury must be satisfied that the Crown had proved their case. I submit that they cannot come to that conclusion.

The prisoner is the victim of circumstances. He is a young man of twenty-five years of age, who has lived a clean life, and is of a charming personality. And the Crown allege that he suddenly ceased to be all that class of boy, and turned into a perfect fiend. There is no motive shown for this sudden change, and it wants some extraordinary evidence to make the jury believe in this sudden change. There is no motive at all. The prisoner was on friendly terms with Neil, but had very little to do with him, as his work on the station was different. The evidence for the Crown is absolutely unreliable, particularly that of Drew and Burdekin. Burdekin's evidence is absolutely untrue.

There are mysteries in this case which I won't attempt to solve…The only people who could have removed that mystery are the police. I regret exceedingly to say that the police made up their mind that only Vernon was guilty. They didn't concern themselves to find out if anyone else was guilty. They did not take the trouble to search Drew's hut or the Chinese camps. They did not take the bats until long after the occurrence, and they did not take Neil's dying depositions at all. Burdekin told his story…Burdekin is lying. There is some motive in Burdekin's lying. I don't know what that motive is.

There had been considerable conjecture as to whether Feez would call on his client to testify. Now he dispelled it: 'I am putting the prisoner in the box.'

*

So, the following morning, the celebrity prisoner commenced his narration in what *Truth* called 'a clear, audible voice, and in a straightforward manner' looking 'very pale, but young and boyish.' George Vernon's account of the day cleaved to those already given, even if it stepped politely round his relations with Neil.

> After tea he had a smoke and went to the men's quarters, saw Drew, and talked to him some time. He had a nip with Drew, and Drew said, 'There's a drink left – it will do for old Neil.' Neil came up and told witness that there was some meat in a sack for his dog. Witness had told Drew that Neil generally had whisky there. He had had a drink with him several times. Witness had never any quarrel with Neil, but did not like him. He took the meat and walked towards the house. He passed Neil, going towards the men's hut, and said 'Good night', to which Neil

replied 'Good night.' That was the last time, that
witness saw Neil until after the occurrence. He
went into the house and wrote a letter to his
grandfather, R. G. Jeffray, in London.

Feez tendered the letter.

Real: Admitted.

Kingsbury: I object.

Real: You should object at the proper time. You
are too late.

The Crown Prosecutor was far too late. George
struck a note of candour in confessing that he'd
taken a drink or three that night; indeed, he
emphasised it.

Witness agreed with the other witnesses in their
account of most of the events of the night, except
that he said that there was much more whisky
drunk. He got two bottles from Higginson's
room and then did not remember anything
more that night as he got 'pretty drunk'. In
the morning he felt 'pretty sick', and went and
got another bottle of whisky, had a nip, and
went down to the kitchen...The next thing he
remembered was Cullen coming into the room.

George had been reluctant to ride for help, he claimed, merely because it had been too dangerous in the dark; in his reference to there being 'no bats between St George and Dirrinbandi', he had simply been exempting the station's, and his, own. Finally Feez led George through a selective synopsis of his life, designed chiefly to position him as 'that class of boy' gone only so slightly awry. 'I was sixteen when my father died, then being on a naval training vessel,' as though aiming for a likeness with the youth in 'Casabianca' ('The boy stood on the burning deck/Whence all but he had fled...'). The *Mail* summed up his self-diagnosis: 'He knew of no trace of insanity or epilepsy in any member of his family. It was not true he suffered from a very irritable temper, and he did not think he was of a nervous disposition. Witness had trouble with the Burdekins on one occasion.' This had involved his asking for some hot water for Higginson, and Burdekin complaining that he was a 'bloody nuisance.' It hardly constituted grounds for a vendetta.

On Wednesday, the defence closed with two highly effective witnesses. The first was the station inspector Thomas Brown, who recounted his conversation with Burdekin on 27 September, where the cook had equivocated about his identification of George in Neil's room. Both Burdekins had been taxed about these exchanges and played them down, but Brown was cogent and plausible.

The case's last witness, hitherto unheralded, made perhaps the most arresting appearance of all. Charles Makeson was an invalid bush worker who had been a patient at St George Hospital since May 1910. He had been in the ward on the morning of Neil's admission, and an earwitness, as it were, to Cullen's interview with the old man. He arrived in court on a stretcher, having made the journey, like James Tolson, at the expense of Australian Pastoral Company, and been accommodated overnight at the Mater Misericordiam Hospital. Now he gave testimony hugely helpful to the company's young English employee.

> Cullen started questioning him. Cullen said, 'Now, are you sure you don't know who did it?' Neil said 'no' most emphatically...Cullen then asked whether he had a row with anybody on

the station and Neil replied that he had not. There was some reference to Neil and Vernon being together that evening and Cullen asked if they had a row. Neil said 'no'...Cullen asked what time Vernon left him and Neil said it was about 9 o'clock. He heard Neil say 'We parted good friends'. There were one or' two questions asked which witness could not recall. The last question he heard was 'You are sure it was not Vernon?' and Neil said 'Nonsense, nonsense; we were much too good friends. Now, drop it for a day or two.'

A sharper prosecutor might have made more of Makeson's evidence. If reliance was to be placed on the testimony, these additional affirmations of Neil's were rather at odds with George's distaste for the old man ('He did not like him') and standoffishness ('He had had no drinks whatever with Neil that night'). In George's recollection, they had exchanged no more than brisk good nights; why would Neil have professed that they were such 'good friends'? But Kingsbury had been overwhelmed by the case; he asked only a few cursory questions before the defence, rather comfortably, rested.

*

Day 12 of what was now Queensland's longest murder trial was dedicated to closing addresses. Feez spoke for more than three hours, beginning with praise for the 'manly and straightforward manner' in which George had given his testament and chronicled his career. With Makeson's evidence fresh, he invoked Neil's deathbed defence of George: 'We were too good friends for Vernon to do such a thing'. George, Feez observed, 'must have changed from a rational young man into a ferocious animal if the story told against him were true'. Sutherland's evidence was a misapprehension, Drew's a hallucination, Burdekin's a fabrication.

> This man Burdekin is embittered against this boy Vernon for some reason or other. Would you believe Burdekin against Vernon? You have heard both in the witness box. It is most remarkable that Burdekin and Drew got Vernon to protect them—this criminal, this dastardly criminal—with a rifle, one knowing (as they swore) Vernon had committed the dastardly deed, and the other suspecting him of the crime. The story against Vernon was

probably started by Burdekin and no effort was made, even by the police, to find out the real perpetrator of the crime.

'Addressed jury for just over 3 hours and I am clear I was effective,' Feez scrawled in his diary. 'Terribly done after it.' But it was Kingsbury who really sounded like he was done. He claimed that the Crown Prosecutor was 'not an advocate under any circumstances', and that

CROWN. PROSECUTOR KINGSBURY.

'if he outlined fairly and fully the evidence that he intended to produce, and that evidence came out as he outlined, it might not be necessary to have anything further to say.' 'Not an advocate'? Nobody missed that Kingsbury was effectively disowning Burdekin. Before his address petered out after roughly half an hour, Real also stepped in with a remark about the possibility of some witnesses in the case having committed 'direct perjury', in which case 'the Crown Prosecutor could have only one duty.' And in his charge the next day before the jury retired at 3.20pm, the judge showed that his earlier reservations about Feez's cross-examination were forgotten. While he continued treating the prosecution case in general favourably, he had to admit that the case's star witness had been a disappointment.

> The credit of Burdekin was impeached, and the Crown Prosecutor had virtually called him a liar. He certainly told a very strange fairy story about his early years. It was very hard to credit such an account. If the tale were false there must be some reason for it. If it were true then it was a very sad one...If the jury deemed the evidence true, they had to find the prisoner guilty, however painful that duty might be. But if they could not believe it – and if as honest men they did not know which to believe – then it was their duty to find him innocent.

Crowds for *R v Vernon* had been building for days. The crowd for the denouement that poured through the Supreme Court's iron gates as they opened just before 11am on Saturday 11 March

1911 was the largest yet. From a public perspective, it would be a great spectacle either way: either a death sentence, with all its attendant ceremonies, or a cheated hangman, with cheers for freedom. By now, the popular preference was for the latter. As George emerged from the cells amid a 'great and painful silence', *Truth* was moved by the 'piteous look' and 'pale drawn face' of 'the accused boy', which showed signs of 'the terrible mental suffering through which he had passed lately'.

> However, when the jury filed into the court, Vernon stood up manfully, and looked steadily at the twelve men who had his life in their hands. After the jurymen's names had been read over, they were asked the usual questions, and when it came to the great question, 'Gentlemen of the jury, do you find the prisoner guilty or not guilty', the silence could be felt painfully. Then, almost before the foreman could open his lips, several jurymen said, 'Not guilty', and the foreman followed with his formal declaration, 'Not guilty'.
>
> Immediately a ripple of irrepressible, spontaneous applause broke out in the gallery, which was immediately repressed. Vernon then

looked steadily at his Honor, who said: 'Is there any other charge against the prisoner?'

Mr. Kingsbury: No, your Honor.

His Honor (to the prisoner): You are discharged.

Immediately the warder opened the door of the dock, Vernon's legal advisers, who have fought so splendidly and against such difficulties, for him, jumped up and went to the dock to congratulate him. At first he stood for a moment dazed, and then collected himself, and walked out of the dock a free man.

Chief among them, of course, was Feez, who had risen from his sickbed after feeling 'very anxious all the evening', and who now had the pleasure of lunch on George Street with his client and attendant boosters. 'Vernon acquitted and thank God as I believe he is innocent,' he concluded in his diary. 'Was over at Lennons with Mr Jeffray, Mr McNaughton and Vernon.' As the foursome walked the short distance to the hotel, they were cheered to the echo; later George and his uncle departed by motorcar for Appin, the Jeffray property in Ascot. For a first time in his scapegrace life, the twenty-five-year-old Englishman savoured the bumper toasts his father had known through cricket.

*

For the Crown, *R v Vernon* was a bitter setback. Kingsbury and Geraghty appeared to have lost an unloseable case; worse, it joined the state's annals of unsolved crime stretching from the Gatton horror to Nellie Duffy's slaying on Carpentaria Downs. In a leader headlined 'Undetected Crimes', the *Daily Mail* took satisfaction in the fact that 'young Vernon now walks about with the freedom that every British subject enjoys, and the consciousness that an impartial jury after a long and patient trial have declared his innocence', while admitting that such satisfaction was circumscribed.

> The trial which attracted an enormous amount of public interest, centred around a crime which was typical of the West and of the bush generally. Nor was it without its dramatic incident as typified by an important witness being brought into court on an ambulance or

hospital stretcher. The singularly able defence by Mr Feez practically removed any fear of the gallows before his Honour's judicious and careful summing up...But while Vernon, after a painful and trying detention of something like six months, has been proved innocent, the Queensland public will hardly be satisfied if Vernon's acquittal is to mean an end to the case. The fact still remains that the old man was fatally murdered...and his murderer still walks the earth...That grim tragedy at Doondi station still remains, and the actual murderer is not only at large but possibly believes that no efforts are being made to bring the crime home to him. Neil's corpse cries for vengeance on his murderer, and the western station mystery must not be relegated to the appalling list of undetected crimes for which Queensland has occasion to blush.

Geraghty was incensed by the editorial, and to Cahill sent a furious rebuttal:

There was abundant direct evidence to show beyond the shadow of a doubt that the accused was guilty of the crime with which he was charged. If the writer of this article had even taken the trouble to carefully read the evidence given at the trial at the Supreme Court he would have found that the evidence supported the charge against the accused. Every person who was at Doondi on the night of the murder with the exception of the accused was called by police as witnesses in the case.

Cahill replied soothingly, commending Geraghty for 'the conscientious and capable manner that has always characterised the performance of your duties', and opining 'that very little blame attaches to any member of the Police Force for want of conscientious effort'. Yet there would be no appeal, and the prevalent note was sounded by *Truth*:

> So happily ended one of the most sensational trials that has ever been known in Queensland; a trial which was intense in its thrilling and absorbing interest; but, apart from its interest, this trial also will afford matter for grave consideration for the people of Queens land. It will give them pause to think whether one at least of our Anglo-Saxon institutions is not seriously defective and faulty; whether the present system of dealing with crimes and the detection of criminals, and bringing the guilty person to conviction, is not wanting...

In the present case there can be no doubt that, under all the circumstances of the case, the police did their duty in arresting Vernon and bringing him to trial. The circumstances surrounding the tragedy at Doondi were helped to appear all against Vernon by the personnel who gave the information to the police; but the duty of the police is not to judge a man. Their plain duty is to investigate thoroughly all the circumstances of the crime, and seek evidence from any quarter from which there is a chance of getting any light on the matter. The question is: Has that been done in the Doondi case? From what transpired at the trial, it appears that it was not done. Everyone was apparently convinced of Vernon's guilt, and, therefore, no one bothered about anything that did not tend to establish his guilt. Consequently, if Vernon had not possessed the means of obtaining effective legal assistance in his extremity, he would have been convicted. "Truth" congratulates his counsel on the ability which they both displayed in this case, and at times under grave difficulties. At the same time, it is rarely that counsel has a case put into their hands so exhaustively and thoroughly prepared as this case was by the solicitors concerned.

There were a range of derisive cartoons, none quite so eye-catching as the cover of the 26 March edition of *Truth*. In 'Waiting for a Clue', 'Public Opinion', adventurously personified by a woman, tapped the shoulder of a slumbering constable: 'Excuse me, am I to hear any more about this Doondi mystery or is it to be put with the others?' It was. But not for long.

Truth

Conducted by JOHN NORTON.

BRISBANE, SUNDAY, MARCH 26. 1911.

Waiting For a Clue.

CRIMES UNSOLVED

DOONDI MURDER

PUBLIC OPINION

PUBLIC OPINION : Excuse me ; am I to hear anything more about this Doondi mystery, or is it to be put with the others ?

7

'I AM THE MAN'

So, on the afternoon of 21 July 1911, George Vernon sat across the desk from Horatio Bottomley, commencing his narrative with a career precis – brief sojourns, enabled by social connections, ended by anti-social indiscretions. He had been back in England about a fortnight, staying with his maternal grandparents, Robert and Margaret Jeffray, and their unmarried daughter Agnes, at 46 Elm Park Road, Chelsea. The euphoria of his acquittal had long worn off. He had resolved in his desperation to do something about his drinking, admitting himself to the Keeley Institute in West Bolton Gardens.

The Institute, a clinic for inebriates named for its entrepeneurial American founder, specialised in injections of a 'gold cure' that actually contained alcohol mixed with a variety of other substances, variously reported as sulphate of strychnine, muriate of ammonia, atropine, apomorphine, aloin, belladonna, hyoscine, scopolamine, opium, and morphine – it was, essentially, useless. Yet through medicalising alcoholism, rather than regarding it a moral deficiency, the treatment also had its successes. The Keeley Institute, noted *The Times* approvingly, did not judge: 'The patients enter of their own free will. The door of the Institute is always open, and the patient can go in and out as it pleases him.' The 'gold cure' would have been no help to George, but the institute policy was why he was free on the day in question.

John Bull had not been his first stop. George had, it would emerge, gone first to Fleet Street, and visited at least two newspapers, possibly more, with the initial idea of selling his story. One of them was the London bureau of Wellington's *New Zealand Times*, to whom he agitatedly explained that his tale 'would create tremendous excitement in Australia.' As a 'special correspondent' recounted, George was to be disappointed.

> The officer in charge, however, was not open to buy the confession on the terms required; indeed, he was not at all anxious to acquire it on any terms, for men who are, on their own confession, desperately hard up, are not usually

too particular as to the mean they adopt to 'raise the wind'. Moreover, Vernon did not seem quite rational. He appeared to be labouring under the influences of drugs or drink, and, truth to tell, his manner generally did not inspire either confidence or courage.

So the interview was cut as short as possible. All that could be gathered was that the young fellow was George Vernon, who was tried for the murder of John Neil at the Doondi Station, Queensland, on September 23rd, 1910, and acquitted; that he really did commit the murder, and that he was anxious to raise money on his confession in order to go with somebody he referred to as 'her' to Canada.

That he really did commit the murder: it was an astounding change of tack. He had protested his innocence loud and long. Friends and family had believed in it; companies had invested in it; well-wishers had cheered it. Yet it was precisely this that in George's mind had made such an asset of the secret of his guilt – one he believed he could sell, having been acquitted, thus being beyond the reach of the law to try again. Had he revealed all to the Jeffrays? Was that why he now desperately needed the money? For having been disappointed at the *New Zealand Times*, he also visited the *Daily Express*, and probably also others. Each time was he turned away. Which is why he wandered down the Strand and Drury Lane bound for Long Acre.

Which is why Bottomley was now taking down George's testament of the night in question: 'Last year I was sent out to Queensland and got a berth on the Doondi Station, belonging to the Australian Pastoral Company, my uncle being chairman of the company. It was on this station that the events of which I am about to speak occurred.' Bottomley did not trouble to check the various spellings; otherwise he seems to have let the testament proceed without interruption.

> On September 23rd last, the manager of the station, Mr. Higginson, was away, and the only persons at the station besides myself were the cook, named Burdikan, and his wife; the gardener, John Neil; a man named Drew; and a half-caste boy called Bourram. About midnight the cook, as he thought, heard cries in Neil's room, which was very near his own, and on going to see what was the matter, found Neil lying between the two beds in a welter of blood,

there being no one else in the room, or within sight. Of course, everybody was immediately aroused. The Chinese store was broken open to get some whisky, and a man rode off for a constable and a doctor.

However, after taking a considerable quantity of whisky I went to my room drunk, and was only aroused next morning about midday, when a constable told me he was arresting me for a brutal outrage on the gardener, Neil. Meantime, Neil had been taken by cart to a hospital at St George's, some 18 miles from the station, where four days later he died. Thereupon I was charged with wilful murder, and on February 10th last [sic] was put on my trial before His Honour the acting Chief Justice, Mr. Justice Real, and a jury. The trial lasted 14 days, and the Public Prosecutor seemed strangely unwilling to press home the evidence against me, but the Judge was dead against him. It should be said that the murdered man stated in his dying deposition that he could not recognise the person who attacked him, but that the weapon was a cricket bat. Ultimately the Jury, after considering the matter for some 18 hours, returned a verdict of "Not guilty", and I became a free man once more. A point in my favour was the evidence that, having regard to the pitch of the room, it would have been difficult for the wounds from which Neil died to have been inflicted with a cricket bat.

This 'pitch of the room' appears to have been a misunderstanding on Bottomley's part – George was probably referring to the visibility of Neil's room from the Burdekins. Indeed it was at this point in the article that *John Bull* would interpolate a line of substantiation: 'Upon looking up the Brisbane papers, we found a full report of the trial and that Vernon's description of it tallied in all substantial particulars with the facts.' This was to prepare the reader for the eye-catching subheading: 'I COMMITTED THE MURDER.'

'Now,' said Vernon, 'I am the man who was in the dock for 13 days and who was acquitted at the end of the trial. As a matter of fact, I committed the murder. It was said by one of the witnesses that on the way from Neil's room to my own I confessed that I had attacked the old man. This I denied at the trial, but it was quite true. At the trial no motive was suggested for the murder, but the facts are these. On the night in question I was with a woman. She was in my room when Neil called for his orders for next day. This was about 9 o'clock in the evening.

At midnight I went over to Neil's room, and I asked him if he intended to tell Mr. Higginson he had seen. I had my cricket bat in my hand, and I said, "Now, look here Jack. Are you going to tell Mr. Higginson this in the morning?"

He said, "Yes, I am. I think it is a damned shame that young fellows like you should take advantage of working men's wives."

I said, "Well, are you quite sure you are going to do this?" "Yes," he said, "quite certain."

"Well, then," I said, "you can go to Hell," and I hit him on the head.

My nerve failed me. I did not hit him hard enough, but I pulled myself together and hit him about ten times, when I thought I had finished him. He was an old man, over sixty years of age. I then set fire to the room and went out. I went over to my own room and found that my pyjamas were smothered in blood, so I wrapped them up in a packet, then put them into some sacking with screws and nails, and threw them into the river just outside my room.

Cherchez la femme, then. On the night in question George Vernon had been caught *in flagrante* with Isabella Burdekin, wife of his chief accuser, that man of 'peculiar disposition' who so resembled 'a ship's steward'. George had let something slip to Drew. Neil had then quite possibly let something slip to Sutherland. But then Neil had clammed up. Geraghty had imagined that Neil was protecting his assailant out of kindness to Arthur Higginson; it was likelier out of kindness to Ralph Burdekin.

Ironically, the cuckold had then helped acquit the co-respondent by being too eager to assist the police, claiming certainty of identification for what had merely been a well-founded suspicion. And, yes, the cricket bat had been the murder weapon – the cricket bat which connected George to G. F., the Ashes veteran father that he had scarcely known, in the cricket bag that had accompanied so optimistically into the wilderness, where there was nobody to play with. George's use of it as a bludgeon may have been the only time he swung it in Australia.

So what now for George Vernon? *John Bull's* next sub-heading read: 'INTENDED FLIGHT'.

Such was the story told to us by Vernon. "Now," said he, "I think that will make fine copy. You can use it and state what I have told you, provided you do not do so for a week. I am sick of things here. I have been at the Keeley Institute ever since I returned to England by the P & O boat a fortnight ago, and I am stuffed full of drink and drugs. I intend to cut myself free of all my relatives and friends and to go with a girl who is very fond of me to British Columbia. What we shall do afterwards does not concern anybody but ourselves."

Before accepting so extraordinary a story we naturally required strong-confirmatory evidence, and this he offered to give us. He showed us a large number of private letters, which bore out his statements in every respect so far as his relations and present intentions were and he reminded us that, as he had been acquitted, we should not be impeding the course of justice by allowing him to leave the country without informing the police.

Who was this girl? Possibly a pre-existing acquaintance, as a fortnight seems a very short time to have struck up sufficient of a bond with someone equally intent on leaving country, although possibly also someone he had met through the Keeley Institute. Interestingly, George refers to severing his other links, with a bitterness towards his former saviours ('I am sick of things here'; 'I intend to cut myself free of all my relatives and friends'): perhaps he had not received the homecoming he'd expected; perhaps he had revealed to them his secret; perhaps he had even been turned out. British Columbia had been his first billet abroad, as a teenage midshipman: returning there smacks of an attempting to turn the clock back. At the same time, George seemed to grasp that this was impossible.

> Vernon seemed greatly distressed after unburdening himself, and in leaving the room he said to us, 'Well, look out for to-morrow's papers.' We did not at the moment pay much attention to this remark, but strongly advised him to return to the Keeley Institute, to remain there until the course of treatment was completed, in the event to do nothing rash, but to communicate with his friends, who, we had no doubt from what he told us, would find the necessary funds to give him a new start in

life. He looked at us in a strange kind of way, and whispered, under his breath, 'Wait till to-morrow, and see.'

But George Vernon's inchoate plans, such as they were, would barely outlast their utterance. Having deposited his macabre tale with Bottomley, George took a journey of which only the destination is known. The Army & Navy Store on Victoria Street, largest in a chain of emporia, was *the* place in London for tailoring, stationery, drapery, pharmaceuticals and fancy goods – also, as befitted what had started as a military cooperative society, small arms, rifles and ammunition. Late in the afternoon, George purchased a revolver from its guns department under a false name, took the short stroll past Westminister Cathedral and the signs for the South Eastern & Chatham Railway, locked a toilet cubicle door behind him at Victoria Station and blew his brains out. In his pocket were found his certificate of discharge from the British South African Police and a letter congratulating him on his acquittal. His body was identified by his aunt Agnes Jeffray and his godfather A. J. Webbe. A short item appeared in *The Times* on Tuesday 25 July 1911.

ARMY & NAVY CO-OPERATIVE SOCIETY, LTD.

105, VICTORIA STREET, WESTMINSTER, LONDON. S.W.

Telephone Nos.

Westminster, 461
(the present—See Special Notice).
Gerrard, 1892
(Box Office only).

Call Offices for Members—
Near Lounge,
5315 Westminster.
In Ladies' Cloak Room,
382 Westminster.

Telegraphic Addresses

"Army, London."
"Army, Plymouth."
"Army, Aldershot."
"Army, Portsmouth."
"Army, Weymouth."
"Armistice, Bombay."
"Armistice, Calcutta."

The STORES are situated within Five Minutes' Walk of VICTORIA STATION, from which Omnibuses run to all parts of London. The St. James's Park Station is within Three Minutes' Walk of, and is almost opposite the Stores.

RULES OF THE SOCIETY
AND
PRICE LIST
OF ARTICLES SOLD AT THE STORES.
No. 85.

15th MARCH, 1908.

LONDON:
PRINTED BY THE ARMY & NAVY CO-OPERATIVE SOCIETY, LIMITED, 105, VICTORIA STREET, WESTMINSTER, S.W.

SUICIDE AT VICTORIA STATION.—An inquest was held at Westminster yesterday concerning the death of George Valentine Jeffray Vernon, aged 25, son of a former Middlesex cricketer, and lately living in Elm Park Road, Chelsea, who shot himself at Victoria Station on Friday. Mr. Alexander J. Webbe, of Eaton Square, Mr. Vernon's godfather, said he was at one time in the South African Police and had been to Canada and Australia. By his own free will he recently entered a home for inebriates in West Fulton Gardens. He had been depressed in regard to his future prospects, and was most anxious to be cured of his drinking habits. Other evidence showed that on Friday, Mr. Vernon purchased a revolver and cartridges at the Army and Navy Stores, giving the name of a cousin, whose name he signed. He then went to Victoria Station (S.E. and C.R.) and later was found shot in a lavatory. The jury returned a verdict of 'Suicide during temporary insanity.'

*

"MURDER WILL OUT!"

A STARTLING CONFESSION BY
AN ACQUITTED MAN

Murder may pass unpunished for a time,
But tardy justice will o'ertake the crime

With invocations of Chaucer and Dryden, *John Bull* proceeded to publish its squalid scoop on 5 August 1911, two weeks after George had walked in, explaining that the young man had 'called upon us and told us the following amazing story, which we reduced to writing and allowed him to sign, as he said it would ease his troubled mind'. Bottomley was unconcerned that it had clearly eased nothing – he also understood that happy facet of the genre of posthumous confession, that its maker was not around to contradict the teller.

Some thought it all a bit convenient. Conspicious by its absence from Bottomley's record of the encounter is any mention of money. George slides from 'easing his troubled mind' to 'great distress' without an intervening step. Not surprisingly, given Bottomley's reputation, this courted some scepticism, including from the *New Zealand Times*.

No mention is made in *John Bull* of any suggestion of payment being made for the confession, yet when he came to your correspondent he was keen on the money he was expecting to get for it. Apparently he thought it was worth many sovereigns, and he spoke of 'twenty or thirty pounds' being enough to take him and person he referred to as 'her' to Canada. Did he confess to *John Bull* under the impression that he would receive a substantial sum, and finding his hopes disappointed resolve upon suicide?

It would explain, at least, the shift in George's tone from shallow boasting to suicide ideation ('Well, wait for to-morrow's papers') – that in his excitement at finding a listener, George had failed to secure payment, then threatened to burden the conscience that Bottomley, frankly, had been born without. The most famous tale of Bottomley concerns his stint in Wormwood Scrubs where he was occupied in the mailbag section. 'Ah, Bottomley, sewing?' a visitor is alleged to have said. 'No,' replied Bottomley. 'Reaping.'

By the time Bottomley had shared George's tale with *John Bull's* half-million readers, George was at least safely buried. Although the Jeffrays registered his death in London's St George Hanover Square, George was interred in an unmarked grave in Binfield Cemetery, Berkshire, near his aunt Helen's country estate. But inevitably, the story spread, and the reaction elsewhere was less scandal than satisfaction. Sergeant Mathias Daley in Roma, for example, clipped the short item that appeared in Brisbane's *Daily Mail* on 14 August ('The Doondi Murder – A Confession in London'), enclosed it in an envelope with the editorial to which the police had taken such exception ('Undetected Crimes'), and posted it to Cahill. 'This was a most trying case for the Police investigating and putting the case together particularly those that came long distances and only reached the scene of the tragedy 10 days after the murder was committed,' he commented, having been especially tried by the loss of a daughter in his absence from home. 'In forwarding the cutting I would respectively beg leave to state that so far as the action of the Police engaged was concerned that this case was conclusive and as clean a case as ever went into a Court.' It was no coincidence who was appointed to succeed Inspector Jack White as chief of Brisbane's Metropolitan Police a few weeks later. The rhyme *Truth* composed to celebrate the appointment of James Geraghty must have had *R v Vernon* in mind.

> Here is the bold Geraghty
> A lad both brave and hearghty
> Who, as the successor of White,
> Will, sure, please every parghty.

Though White was white, as we all know,
Geraghty wants but time to show
To all the clever coves who know,
He's up to every smarghty.

George Vernon's fate made newspapers as far afield as the US, Canada and New Zealand, but obviously the nearer the crime the sharper the response. *Truth* indulged in a comprehensive recapitulation beneath a four-tier headline.

THE DOONDI MURDER
Battler Battered to Death on the Banks of the Balonne
QUEER QUEENSLAND CASE RESUSCITATED
Accused Tried and Acquitted, Confesses and Commits Suicide

St George's own *Balonne Beacon*, which had reported the committal hearing comprehensively, could scarce forebear to cheer:

> Vernon was a young man, well connected, who led a wandering life, and right through a trying period bore himself almost with bravado, and never for a moment weakening. At the time,

knowing in his own heart that he was guilty, and that he would likely receive the sentence of death, the strain of the prolonged murder trial must have been severe. But after defeating the ends of justice, and the saving of his neck and life, the reaction set in. That little invisible thing called conscience, supposed to be included in the anatomy of every person, commenced its dreadful work, and to such purpose that, when the murderer was several thousands miles from the scene of his wrongdoing, he confessed his guilt, afterwards paid the full penalty by his own hand for the crime he committed. So ends the Doondi murder case, sensational to the last!

Not quite last. Like even the most temporary sensations, *R v Vernon* had an afterlife, sustained by association as well as legend. 'He leapt into limelight at the time by his skilful handling of the Doondi tragedy case wherein he appeared on behalf of the accused,' said *Truth* in tributing 'Barrister A. H. H. M. Feez KC' in October 1923. 'The defendant young Englishman, "scion of a noble house", was, with the aid of the oratorical powers of Mr Feez, acquitted. Judges and jury discharged him without a stain on his character.

Later in England the young man confessed his guilt to the notorious Horatio Bottomley and then suicided.' A rum-soaked murder involving two labourers on Narine Station the following month caused *Truth* to invoke 'the sensational Doondi murder', where 'it will be remembered that the horror was the outcome of a drunken spree.'

As events receded into memory, they also blurred. In December 1919, the veteran China correspondent of *The Times*, G. E. ('Chinese') Morrison received a letter from his gossipy masseur Arthur Robertson outlining the murder, and identifying George as the son of 'the cricketer G. F. Vernon', but adding a fantastical twist: 'By dextrous defence the blame was fixed to an Australian black fellow who was found guilty by a prejudiced jury and hanged.' A 1968 history of the shire of Balonne suggests that Doondi's dark past was still the subject of local talk half a century later, jest having entered the retelling:

> It appears that the book-keeper [sic] at the station, old Jack Neal [sic], was at variance with 'a pommy jackeroo' for having reported some missing bottles of rum from the store. Later

old Jack was discovered in a dying state, it being alleged that the murder weapon was a cricket bat, and the 'pommy owned a bat. Old Jack was certainly hit for six. A jury found the 'pommy' not guilty and he returned to his homeland with the score at one not out. Rumours, which is a fickle dame, had it that the 'pommy' later confessed to the crime and committed suicide. He came to Australia for colonial experience, but it looks as if the wrong man got it.

The 'Doondi Station Tragedy' has not, in the end, found itself a secure place in Australian crime's bloody pageant. George's notability as the 'scion of a noble house' was inherently perishable. The killer was merely a hot-headed wastrel not a bloody mutilator or wintry psychopath. The victim was only an old man, not a beautiful woman or an innocent child. The murder method was basic, the murder weapon crude. Until Luke Batty's tragic death at the hands of his estranged father Greg Anderson in February 2014, few Australian killers had exploited the cricket bat's lethal potential.

The *deus ex machina* of the post-acquittal confession, moreover, is of a very particular, even

Doondi Station today

somewhat unappealing, kind. George Vernon bears little resemblance to any of fiction's great guilty consciences. He is no Raskolnikov in *Crime and Punishment* or Laurent in *Thérèse Raquin*. While we are dependent on Bottomley's stenography, George appeared at their encounter to manifest neither regret nor contrition where John Neil was concerned. He reproached himself for clumsiness ('My nerve failed me'), praised himself for nerve ('I am the man who was in the dock for thirteen days'). He offered no atonement, sought no absolution, and wanted, primarily, money.

'When murderers shut deeds close, this curse does seal 'em:/If none disclose 'em, they themselves reveal 'em!' Thus Thomas Middleton's famous couplet in the Jacobean playwright's *The Revenger's Tragedy*. Yet, criminologically, this is very seldom true. The most famous instance of an unstable conscience is probably Constance Kent, the Road Hill House murderer of 1860, who confided in a clergyman. But Kent was sixteen, intensely religious and highly suggestible, and Kate Summerscale conjectures in *The Suspicions of Mister Whicher* (2008) that her revelations were not comprehensive. Unbidden confession to murder, as distinct from assisted, coerced and negotiated, is scarcely known. Even the US, that sanguinary encyclopaedia of murder, offers few examples: there was Mack Ray Edwards, a compulsive child killer who in 1970 turned himself in and took his own life in San Quentin the following year; there is Wayne Adam Ford, an ephebophilic prostitute killer still on death row in San Quentin after presenting himself to police in 1998. But few are the tell-tale hearts that beat beneath floorboards.

Still, the verdict of temporary insanity on George does not quite suffice. Self-destruction might be the ultimate extremity, but it usually follows a path of reasoning, however tortured. Was confession a revenge on those, including his father, who had since his mother's death been so little able to find anything to do with him? Was suicide a final demand for recognition from those who had simply grown accustomed to sending him away? Suicide has been described as a permanent solution to a temporary problem. But to George, abandoned, angry, doomed to ricochet round an unfeeling empire, it would have seemed at that moment like a perfectly rational appraisal of his prospects. The moon had fallen. Only darkness remained.

A GUIDE TO SOURCES

Things being as they were, *The Night was a Bright Moonlight and I Could See a Man Quite Plain* was researched and composed almost entirely at my desk with either Trove, Ancestry, British Newspaper Archive, Newspapers.com, my email or some faraway catalogue open infront of me. But I had some generous help along the way from, inter alia, Hector and Ian Munro (from the Clan Munro in Scotland), Peter Applegarth and Glenn Martin (judges of the Supreme Court of Queensland), Professor Marjory Harper (chair of history at the University of Aberdeen), and the indefatigable Graeme Haigh (of Grajohn Geneaological Services).

Thanks also to David Studham and Trevor Ruddell at the Melbourne Cricket Club Library; Joanne Seccombe, Senior Reference Archivist at Queensland State Archives; to Jennifer Freeman, reference librarian at the State Library of Queensland; Duncan Leask of the Queensland Police Museum; Angelique Williams, Katie Haden and Katee Dean from the library at the Supreme

Court of Queensland. Gillian Rickard pored over the papers of LadyDarnley in the Medway Archives Centre in England, to no avail, but, naturally, I had to know if I was missing something. I was also pleased to make the acquaintance of Tracey and Stuart Armstrong, owners of Doondi Station since 1994, who sent the lovely overhead image of the property today.

My partner Caroline Overington and my mother Isabel Haigh provided love, enthusiasm and excellent proof reading; my friend Anne-Marie Reeves threw herself into the beguiling design; my friend Russell Jackson helped with what Bishan Bedi calls 'The Twitter' ('Gideon! Are you on The Twitter?!' To which the answer is still no).

This is the inaugural publication of the Archives Liberation Front, colophon designed by my daughter Cecilia Haigh. Our motto was originated earlier this year during a successful campaign for emergency funding for the National Archives of Australia: *Quia solo esse liber files* ('Files just want to be free').

NATIONAL ARCHIVES UK, KEW

Admiralty, Executive Officer Service
ADM 196/50/242 George Valentine Jeffray Vernon

QUEENSLAND POLICE MUSEUM

Police Service Records
4767 Cullen, Thomas Joseph 3698 Daley, Mathias
2761 Dyer, Robert Thomas 2906 Geraghty, James Francis
2448 McGuire, John Duncan 4332 Quinlan, Denis McKeat

QUEENSLAND STATE ARCHIVES

ITM2931 Register of male prisoners admitted (with
descriptions) – HM Prison, Brisbane (Boggo Road),
27/02/1909 – 10/01/1911 [*George Vernon, No.1329*]
ITM27007 Doondi Station 01/04/1888 – 31/12/1930
ITM665840, File number: 8N, John Neil, 27/09/1910–
15/12/1911
ITM2768580 Application Granted for License to be
Counsel for George Vernon – Arthur Herman
Henry Milford Feez, 27/01/1911, No.12 p.9.

STATE LIBRARY OF QUEENSLAND

Australian Pastoral Company Records 1894–1952
Series 62 Box 1570 Letter book volume 14 (OM62/14)
10/7/1909 – 5/9/1910, volume 15 (OM62/15)
2/9/1910 – 15/9/1911

SUPREME COURT OF QUEENSLAND LIBRARY

Diaries of Arthur Feez KC 1910–1911

SELECT BIBLIOGRAPHY

Armstrong, Geoffrey, *In Mitchell's Footsteps: a history of the Balonne Shire*, Smith & Patterson, Brisbane, 1968

Belloc, Hillaire, *Cautionary Tales for Children*, Eveleigh Nash, London, 1907

Berry, Scyld and Rupert Peploe, *Cricket's Burning Passion: Ivo Bligh and the Story of the Ashes*, Methuen, London, 2006

Bryce, James, *Impressions of South Africa*, Macmillan & Co, London, 1897

Coldham, James P., *Lord Hawke: a cricketing biography*, Crowood, Marlborough, 1990

Dunae, Patrick, *Gentlemen Emigrants: From the British Public Schools to the Canadian Frontier*, Douglas & Macintyre, Vancouver, 1981

Felstead, S, Theodore, *Horatio Bottomley: biography of an outstanding personality*, J. Murray, London, 1936

French, Doris, *Ishbel and the Empire: A Biography of Lady Aberdeen*, Dundum Press, Toronto, 1988

Gibbs, Peter and Hugh Phillips, *The History of the British South African Police*, Something of Value, North Ringwood, 1972

Gould, Nat, *The Miner's Cup: a Coolgardie Romance*, George Rutledge, London, 1896

Hartford, George Bibby, *Commander RN*, Arrowsmith, London, 1927

Hawke, Lord, *Recollections and Reminiscences*, Williams & Norgate, London, 1924

Houston, Henry, *The Real Horatio Bottomley*, Hurst & Blackett, London, 1923

Johnston, W. Ross, *The Long Blue Line: a history of the Queensland Police*, Boolarong, Brisbane, 1992

Jones, Mary (editor), *A Life Cut Short: The Edited Letters of Lieutenant Commander Ralph Lyall Clayton*, Persona Naval Press – available on the PNP website (https://www.personanavalpress.co.uk)

Lansbury, Coral, *Arcady in Australia: The Evocation of Australia in Nineteenth-Century English Literature*, Melbourne University Press, Melbourne, 1970

Middleton, Thomas, *The Revenger's Tragedy*, The Arden Shakespeare, London, 2018

O'Sullivan, Thomas, *Sketch of the career of Honorable Patrick Real, late Senior Puisne Judge of the Supreme Court of Queensland*, self-published, Brisbane, 1941

Pearl, Cyril, *Morrison of Peking*, Penguin, Ringwood, 1967

Powell-Williams, *Cold Burial: A True Story of Endurance and Disaster*, St Martin's Griffin, New York, 2002

Pratt, Ambrose, *The Remittance Man*, Ward Lock, London, 1907

Sim, Jack, *History of Boggo Road Gaol 1883–1999*, Jack Sim Publications, Sunnybank Chase, 2018

Stevenson, Robert Louis, *The Wrecker*, Cassell, London, 1899

Summerscale, Kate, *The Suspicions of Mr Whicher: Murder at Road Hill House*, Bloomsbury, London 2008

Symons, Julian, *Horatio Bottomley: a Biography*, Cresset, London, 1955

Twain, Mark, *Following the Equator: a Journey Around the World*, American Publishing Company, Hartford, 1897

Wilde, Oscar, *The Importance of Being Earnest*, Leonard Smithers, London, 1899

Zuelkhe, Mark, *Scoundrels, Dreamers & Second Sons: British Remittance Men in the Canadian West*, Whitecap Cooks, Toronto, 1994

About the Author

Gideon Haigh has been a journalist for almost four decades, published more than 40 books and contributed to more than 100 newspapers and magazines. His cricket books include *The Cricket War*, *The Summer Game* and *On Warne*; his other works span business, medicine, media, social history and true crime. His books *Asbestos House: The Secret History of James Hardie Industries* and *The Office: A Hardworking History* won multiple non-fiction awards. His most recent book is the acclaimed *The Brilliant Boy: Doc Evatt and the Great Australian Dissent*. He lives in Melbourne.